Turning Water Into Wine

PASTOR KEVIN THORPE

Turning Water Into Wine. Copyright 2025 by Pastor Kevin Thorpe. All rights reserved. No part of this publication may be reproduced, distributed, or transmitted in any form or by any means, including photocopying, recording, or other electronic or mechanical methods, without the prior written permission of the publisher, except in the case of brief quotations embodied in critical reviews and certain other noncommercial uses permitted by copyright law.

For permission requests, write to the publisher, addressed "Attention: Permissions Coordinator," 205 N. Michigan Avenue, Suite #810, Chicago, IL 60601. 13th & Joan books may be purchased for educational, business or sales promotional use. For information, please email the Sales Department at sales@13thandjoan.com.

Printed in the U. S. A.

First Printing, February 2025.

Library of Congress Cataloging-in-Publication Data has been applied for.

Dedication

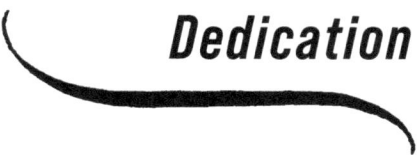

I dedicate this book to all those like me who tried and ultimately failed at making a marriage work. My message to you is that God majors in second chances. If you let Him, He can still turn your water into wine.

Epigraph

Often, we don't want to talk about what we had to go through to get where we are.

What lessons can be learned from running out of wine?

Here's the first thing I want to share with you, and I'm speaking to married people specifically.

Recognize this: It is possible to run out of wine.

Pastor Thorpe

Acknowledgments

TO MY BELOVED WIFE AND LIFE PARTNER, Phoenicha J. Thorpe: When I began this writing journey, you and I were the best of friends. Never in a million years did I foresee that we would ever become more than that, but you did. Thank you for managing our friendship so well and for helping me to make the transition from divorcee to husband. Thank you for your steadfast support and cooperation. Your life and commitment will be an inspiration to many and will provide guidance to others on how to wait on God and how to be ready when God moves. Through our love and union, God has opened so many doors, not the least being the birth of our baby boy, Kevin W. Thorpe, Jr., on April 3, 2024. I can't wait to tell him all the stories of how we met, married, and celebrated God's promise of his arrival. I love you endlessly!

To my divine Faith Church Family: You stood by me through struggle, separation, divorce, and remarriage. You prayed for me while abstaining from the temptation of judging and shunning me. You respected me and continued to trust me as God and I navigated through my uncharted territory. I will never forget you and the impact you continue to make on my life.

To my mother, siblings, nieces, and nephews: I would be nothing without you. You are my "first family." You each have poured so much into me in your own special ways.

To my beloved father, Slater Thorpe Sr., and to my beloved pastor, Reverend Dr. David A Lattimore Jr., who both now exist in the presence of the angels and around the throne of our Heavenly Father: Your words and exemplary lives continue to breathe life and exist in me and all those I am privileged to touch.

CONTENTS

Dedication iii
Epigraph v
Acknowledgments vii
Preface 1
Introduction 3

Pillar 1 7
Pillar 2 27
Pillar 3 41
Pillar 4 51
Pillar 5 61
Pillar 6 69
Pillar 7 79
Pillar 8 91
Pillar 9 99
Pillar 10 111
Pillar 11 119
Pillar 12 131

Conclusion 143
Afterword: A Recipe for Marriage 145
About the Author 159

Preface

WHEN I STARTED WRITING THIS BOOK, it was without having true love in mind for myself. I just wanted to help other couples who were on the verge of divorce but didn't know it, or those who had gotten divorced and needed to look back over the relationship and perform a spiritual autopsy to figure out what happened to tarnish the love once shared.

My first marriage ending made me think about all that went wrong. Dissecting that relationship and thinking about issues I had chosen to avoid and how they became insurmountable hurdles in the relationship made me understand how other people in the world must be doing the same thing. People are staying in relationships that should end or are ignoring the causes of their relationship ending. To continue as a healthy couple, you must look at your relationship's status regularly. If you want to get into a new relationship, you need to know what went wrong in your last relationship, but people do not do either of these difficult evaluations.

What I am hoping is that through a discussion of my relationship, my analysis, and the candid exposure of the immaturity I had when I entered the relationship prior to my first marriage, I will be able to help others learn from me and avoid the pain I went through. Everyone likes to think they understand relationships and know what they are doing but when the breakup happens, they ask themselves what went wrong. Knowing people go through this, I have felt led to be vulnerable and write this book so that others can ask the right questions, protect their relationships, and have a God-honoring marriage.

Introduction

WHEN I PROPOSED TO MY FIRST WIFE, I never would have imagined our relationship would end in divorce. When I chose to propose to her, it was with the understanding that I would be with this woman for the rest of my life. Divorce was not a word in my vocabulary. When things began going wrong in my marriage, the idea that divorce was no longer an idea that applied to other people but was something that may become part of my life story shocked me.

I am a pastor who believes in the word of the Lord. I believe in what He says in the Bible and am quite familiar with the scriptures regarding divorce. In Matthew chapter 5, we are told that sexual immorality, meaning adultery, is a valid reason for divorce. Some are convinced that divorcing for any other reason is a sin. I believe there are other reasons, specifically if a spouse fails to fulfill their role as explained in other New Testament scriptures found in Ephesians chapter 5. Of course, I did everything I could do to avoid divorce but realized that my best efforts were not going to be enough to salvage my marriage.

Now, I will not lie: The idea of actually going through a divorce was not only a challenge emotionally and logistically but also from a biblical perspective. My understanding of the Bible was probably a main factor in why my first marriage lasted as long as it did. The idea that I would be breaking the covenant I made before God with my first wife ate me up on the inside. But at some point, I understood that our staying together in the marriage was not good for either me or my spouse. It was breaking us down both mentally and emotionally, and remaining together would have been detrimental.

Once I proceeded with the divorce and it was official, I spent some time grappling with the ramifications of what I did. Not only was I a Christian who got divorced, but I was also a pastor. How was anyone going to listen to a man who many would believe, from a biblical perspective, sinned? I had to reconcile that fact to my ongoing ministry. I had to understand that there would be people who would not accept and would never understand why I chose to divorce.

I was a broken man living a lie in front of the members of my church, and they did not deserve that. I was not honoring God by standing before them as a hypocrite pretending to be happily married. I am sure on more occasions than one, it was clear on my face that I was going through a rough time. My members are some of the most dedicated and loving people you will come across, and I know that they wanted me to be happy. I could not preach the joy of the Lord when I was not experiencing it but rather living with enormous and increasing stress. My hope was that my congregation would be able to let go of whatever beliefs they held about divorce and put my happiness at the forefront.

So I reconciled with the fact that I needed to be happy. People around me wanted me to be happy and most importantly, God wanted me to be happy. I also realized that I was not a lesser pastor because I was divorced. God's word still guided my life and was my passion as I remained His messenger. I also firmly believed that God still had good things in store for me and wanted me to pass on the message of love and redemption. My trials created an even stronger testimony as I was empowered to minister to couples in a way I never would have envisioned prior to experiencing the pain associated with divorce.

Once I embraced this thinking, I realized that being divorced presented me with an opportunity to tell my members what not to do as they worked to build or maintain a strong and healthy relationship with their spouse.

I tackled the topic of divorce in a sermon taken from the New Testament when Jesus performed His first miracle of turning water into wine. I shared with my congregation the truth revealed in that moment when Christ took ordinary water and made it into spectacular wine.

Just as there was not enough wine at the wedding, marriages can and do run dry. And just as our Savior made a way for the couple at their wedding to celebrate their union, He can and He will walk with us through relationship troubles, including marriages that end in divorce. He can and He will restore us, as you will see in reading about my journey through a divorce to remarry and become a father.

My prayer is that this book will encourage and inspire all who are struggling in a relationship to see, understand, and believe that Christ can turn their water into wine.

PILLAR 1

Keep Jesus at the party.
Pastor Thorpe

THE TITLE OF THIS BOOK ties to the sermon I delivered to my congregation regarding relationships and what the miracle of Christ turning water into wine teaches couples. The message is shared below to provide context for the remainder of the book.

What happens if the water doesn't turn into wine?

Every year in the month of February for the past 22 years that I've served as the pastor of this Faith Church, you could count on me to preach a message about love and relationships. This upcoming week in our culture on the 14th, which is Friday, in case you forgot it is Valentine's Day. So normally, I talk to folks about their "boo thing." Today is a slightly different day. I want to address perhaps the most forgotten group of people in the world: Those who genuinely tried to make their marriages work but somehow their marriage ended up in separation or divorce.

Perhaps the most unministered group in the entire world are men and women who have gone through separation or divorce, even though it is prevalent and affects many. If I were to ask for a show of hands, but I will not, you would see how many would be raised to identify with the fact that they were either directly or indirectly affected by this issue of divorce. I'm talking about people who meant well, who did all that they could to hold it together, and somehow "the wine still ran out." When the wine ran out, even with Jesus and water present, the water still didn't turn into wine. I want to minister to people who tried and still failed. I want to breathe life into your heart and into your mind on how to handle life even when the water doesn't turn into wine.

John chapter 2 records the first miracle that Jesus ever performed. Jesus was invited to a wedding in a city called Cana of Galilee. His mother was there and His disciples were also there. In antiquity, Jewish wedding ceremonies lasted longer than 30 minutes. It was actually a seven-day celebration. The ceremony would occur initially and then seven days of celebrating. It was a major function and a major affair. One of the key elements that had to be present at the seven-day wedding celebration was wine. To not have wine would be like going to Thanksgiving dinner and not finding a turkey on the table. It was a common staple, a common element that was present at every wedding celebration. There had to be wine.

At this wedding though, they ran out of wine. Most scholars believe that the reason Mary attended this wedding is because she was related to the groom. When the servants recognized that they were running out of wine, they went to Mary as a family member. They said to her, "This party is about to be shut down." The maximum level of embarrassment that could be brought to a family was if you had a party, specifically a wedding celebration, and you ran out of wine.

The servants go to Jesus' mother. They say to her, "We were running out of wine." She goes to Jesus and says to him, "Our family is about to experience maximum embarrassment." Jesus' response can be read in the King James Version. He says, "Woman, what have I to do with thee?" The New American Standard and Message Bible says, and I'm paraphrasing, "That's none of my business. That's none of your business." Mary immediately turns to the servants who came to her to tell her that the wine was running out. She says to them, "Whatever He tells you to do, do it." That's an enigma in and of itself about

Mary. Jesus had shut her down, but there was something about the look He had on His face WHEN He shut her down that informed her next move. Mary recognized that it was not a denial and it was only a delay. It was simply a challenge to her faith. She says to the servants, "I don't know WHAT He's going to do, but whatever He tells you to do, do it."

Jesus said, "Those six water pots that you all have, that you have been using for the ceremonial washing of your hands, get new water and fill the pots back up to the top." They went and filled the pots back up to the brims. Jesus said, "Now dip out of the pot and take whatever you dip to the head waiter and let him taste it." When the head waiter took a sip of what had been transformed by Jesus, he called to the bridegroom. He said, "Man, when we planned this party, we orchestrated that we would serve the good wine first and then we would go and bring out the Boone's Farm, the Old Manischewitz, the MD 2020.

The head waiter said to the bridegroom, "You have saved the best for last," which means the water that Jesus turned into wine tasted better than the finest wine that they had been serving for the last seven days.

When I look at this familiar passage in an unfamiliar way, one of the questions I've wrestled with is why did they run out of wine in the first place? So if I was breaking this message into pieces, that would have to be the first piece.

I. The reasons you may have run out of wine. I want to give you some practical reasons that the wine may have run out at this party. Then I want to reverse it and apply them to family and relationships.

So let me give you the first possibility as to why they may have run out of wine.

1. Maybe somebody ordered too little. Maybe somebody didn't properly estimate the crowd size. That's one reason they could have run out of wine. They just didn't order enough.

Let me give you a second reason that they could have run out of wine.

2. Somebody drank too much. Some of you know what it's like to plan an event and somebody tells you that they're going to come alone and then they bring three or four people with them. It's also true that some folks are more thirsty than other folks and eat and drink up all the stuff you've prepared. I've gone to events where it was a buffet but they still have people serving you in the buffet line. They sliced the roast beef so thin that when they cut it off, it was thin enough for me to see through it. The message they were trying to send was, "Well, we see all these folks in here, and we want to make sure that everybody gets a piece." At this wedding, maybe they ran out of wine because of overconsumption. Some people simply drank more than what was customary for an individual to drink.

Maybe they ordered too little. Maybe somebody drank too much. Here's a third possibility.

3. Maybe somebody destroyed some of the bottles. Perhaps when the servants were in the back preparing to unload a case of wine they dropped some of the cases.

These are all very practical, and realistic reasons they could have run out of wine prematurely. Please keep in mind that this was not a sham wedding or a celebration that had been thrown together. They had money, a successful bride, a noble groom, and a loving and supportive family. They had attentive servants and a capable and professional head waiter, but they still ran out of wine.

I want to minister to people who have dealt with separation and divorce to prick something in your heart to help you understand why you may have ended up in divorce in the first place.

The first reason to consider is perhaps when you selected a spouse, maybe you "ordered too little." Let me give you another word for that. It is the word incompatibility. Maybe you married someone and at the time, they could handle who you were. Over time, they just couldn't handle who you became. That's God's word to some single folks in here. You have your eye on Mr. or Mrs. Right and you think they are the one. The reason you need supernatural wisdom when making lifelong decisions is because where you are now is not where you will always be. When you choose a life partner, you have to let God show you who that partner is. The reason is because the one that God has for you can handle where you are and can grow with you as you make it to where you're going. The reason that some folks just didn't work out is because of incompatibility. You didn't order "enough" wine. You needed an extra large and you got an extra small. Maybe somebody ordered too little but then you should also consider that maybe somebody drank too much.

Could it be that the reason your relationship ended up in separation or divorce is because sometimes we take people for granted? You know another word for that? It's neglect. You thought the grass was greener on the other side of the fence but when you got over there, you discovered it was AstroTurf. Somebody drank too much and found themselves in a place of neglect. Someone took the other person for granted, made too many withdrawals without making enough deposits.

But then you should also consider that maybe somebody destroyed some of the bottles. This means there are elements and circumstances in life that can attack a marriage even while you're doing the very best that you can to make it work. Sometimes there are forces beyond your control because you can only control what YOU do. You can't control what the other person does. "Pastor, do you have some examples?" Yes, I do. Infidelity. Having an unfaithful spouse is beyond your control.

Maybe abuse was present. Keep in mind that abuse comes in a number of different forms and any one of them can turn a marriage into a prison that God may have seen fit to free you from. The Church, historically, has failed a number of people by suggesting and even mandating that you should stay in an abusive relationship simply because no form of infidelity has taken place. A more careful and realistic understanding of the scriptures gives rise to the fact that infidelity is not the only justifiable reason that a person should entertain the notion of separation or divorce. Notice what Paul teaches that husbands and wives should expect from their spouse. It reads like this in Ephesians 5:22-33 from The Message Bible.

> *Wives, understand and support your husbands in ways that show your support for Christ. The husband provides leadership to his wife the way Christ does to his church, not by domineering but by cherishing. So just as the church*

submits to Christ as he exercises such leadership, wives should likewise submit to their husbands. Husbands, go all out in your love for your wives, exactly as Christ did for the church—a love marked by giving, not getting. Christ's love makes the church whole. His words evoke her beauty. Everything he does and says is designed to bring the best out of her, dressing her in dazzling white silk, radiant with holiness. And that is how husbands ought to love their wives. They're really doing themselves a favor—since they're already "one" in marriage. No one abuses his own body, does he? No, he feeds and pampers it. That's how Christ treats us, the church, since we are part of his body, And this is why a man leaves father and mother and cherishes his wife. No longer two, they become "one flesh." This is a huge mystery, and I don't pretend to understand it all. What is clearest to me is the way Christ treats the church. And this provides a good picture of how each husband is to treat his wife, loving himself in loving her, and how each wife is to honor her husband."

The relevant question then becomes, what happens when you are married to someone who refuses to "BE" any one of the things that Jesus taught that they should "BE?" How many spouses are there, and there are some, who will narrowly define separation and divorce by infidelity only? Spouses who actually tell the abused or neglected spouse, "You can never leave me because I will never cheat on you." That kind of relationship can become a type of prison. And if you find yourself locked in one, you should seek God's guidance on what your next move may be.

Here's another example of the wine running out due to the destruction of some of the bottles. Abandonment. Paul addresses this in I Corinthians 7:15 in The Message Bible.

> On the other hand, if the unbelieving spouse walks out, you've got to let him or her go. You don't have to hold on desperately. God has called us to make the best of it, as peacefully as we can.

Here's why I raise the issues to the Christian community. Often we vilify, demonize, belittle, and even re-victimize people who ended up in separation or divorce when the real truth is they were faced with circumstances beyond their control. My goal today is very specific. I want to breathe new life back into those, as the hymn writer says, who "tried and failed in your trying!"

You didn't plan on running out of wine but you did because maybe you ordered too little, maybe somebody drank too much, or maybe somebody destroyed some of the bottles.

Well, I don't want to leave you there. I want to push you one step further and talk about lessons learned from running out of wine. It's bad enough to go through it but worse when you go through and don't learn from it. Perhaps we could save a lot of marriages if we talked more about what we learned from what didn't work. Many people are in successful relationships now, but we are rarely or never transparent about what you had to go through to get where you are now. I want to encourage people because some of you are looking for somebody or seeking to be in a healthy and lifelong relationship. There's nothing at all wrong with that. Quite honestly, you're looking for somebody everywhere you go. You're questioning The Lord about everything. "Lord is that him?" Some folks say, "Lord, if that isn't him, make it him."

Often, we don't want to talk about what we had to go through to get where we are. What lessons can be learned from running out of wine? Here's the first thing I want to share with you. I'm speaking to married people specifically at this point. Recognize this: It is possible to run out of wine. The reason, especially with saved or Christian folk that we often miss out on things, is because we can't identify what "may" happen.

If someone would've told me in 1993 when I got married at the age of 20 years old that nearly 21 years later in 2014 my marriage would end in divorce, I would have told them, "You have lost your mind," because I knew that I had done the right thing the correct way. It was going to last forever, only to discover that the wine would run out. Even with your best intentions and your best-laid plan, the wine can run out. Don't miss this. I'm not talking about choices you make or things that you do. I'm talking about something that can happen to you. Things like infidelity, abuse, neglect, and abandonment.

For example, there is a strong word about immature emotional and psychological abuse that occurred in the life of King David, who himself was not a saint. In II Samuel 6, David returned home after scoring a great victory for God. He even danced before the Lord with all of his might until his heavy outer garments were removed, though his undergarments and base garments were still intact. The entire nation was rejoicing with him. That is, everyone except his wife. She berated him for his actions and accused him of being "loose" and provocative as it related to the women who were present as he danced. David stood his ground and declared that it was for the Lord's glory that he was dancing and that before he would take any of it back, he would add more to it! As a consequence, God closed up the womb of David's wife and she remained that way forever.

Let me breathe a strong word to couples. Before I share it, pause and take a deep breath. Ask yourself, "Does this apply to me?" **If your spouse is begging you to fix something, listen to them.**

There are several Greek words for love that are used in classical language. One of them is agape. That's the form of love that God has for us. It is an everlasting love. It will never change. Say it with me. The first love is Agape, A-G-A-P-E. The second form of love is storge, S-T-O-R-G-E. That's the kind of love that parents have for their children and children for their parents. It ought to be an everlasting love. Even if your child is mischievous, you still love him. Even though your parents may not have been perfect, you still love them, and "then you look like them too." Trust me, the older you get, the more you look like them. Before long, if you aren't careful, you'll start acting like them.

Then there's a third form of love. It is philia. That's why the city of Philadelphia is called the city of brotherly love. That's the love that brothers and sisters have for each other or the love that exists between friends. It is a strong love, it can be an everlasting love. There's another Greek word for love. It is the word eros, E-R-O-S. It is where we get our English word, erotic. It is a romantic form of love.

As a reminder here are at least four Greek words that describe love: Agape, storge, philia, and eros. Agape is the love that God has for us. Storge is the love that parents have for their children. Philia is the love you have for your friend. Eros is the love you have for your boo thing.

Here's what I want to warn you about. **Eros can die.** What I never counted on is, while I will always love the former Mrs. Thorpe with the love of God, that's agape. But the part of me that loved her as a husband died. It was not suicide, it was homicide. This was the pivotal moment that changed everything, the reality that caught me completely off guard. We didn't "fall out of love" or "grow apart" as you often hear people report. This was something much deeper. It didn't kill itself, it was murdered. Circumstances killed it.

What I want to share with you is that you may be dealing with some circumstances that you refuse to face, without fully understanding that either your love for them or their love for you is on life support. If you're not careful, it will die. You can look right at them, love them with the love of God, but you just don't feel the same toward them. The word that I breathe to husbands and wives is that if your spouse is begging you to get something straight, listen to them before it's too late.

"Pastor Thorpe, how can I know if I'm getting close?" I'm glad you asked. One way you can know your love is on life support is when the "fight" dies down. See, because right now, you and your spouse may fight all the time because one is constantly trying to pull the other one in a different direction and you fight all the time. Here's what I want to warn you of. If you are not careful, a day is going to come when they won't want to fight anymore. You keep pushing the same buttons, but you won't always get the same result. You think you've won when the reality is their love for you is about to die and you are about to lose. Hey, you can tell when the fight dies down.

Here's the second way you can tell you're on life support: When the "caring" slows down. Right now you might be fighting over what you all are going to have for dinner and you fight about it all the time. If you're not careful, a day will come and he or she will say, "I don't care what you fix. It really doesn't matter that much to me anymore." The caring slows down. You go to work, all big, bad, and bold and even announce to others, "I run everything in my house. Everybody gets quiet when I come home." That isn't out of respect. They just can't stand you. They just don't care like they used to care. You keep pushing the same buttons and have not recognized that you are no longer getting the response that you used to get because the caring has slowed down.

So the first way you know you are on life support is when the fight dies down. Second, caring slows down.

Here's number three: When the "coping" heats up. If they get off at 5, work 15 minutes from the house, but don't come home until 9 when they know you are getting ready to go to bed, it's because they have developed a coping mechanism. The coping mechanism is if they don't have to talk to you. If they don't have to see you. If they don't have to fight with you. They just deal with it by becoming absent. It's called a coping mechanism. Now, when you fight they say, "You know what? You're right. The way you see it, that's exactly what it is. Whatever it is you're thinking, you're on it. That's it." They develop a coping mechanism. There's a danger in coping mechanisms because the further you drift away from the one you love, it may push you in the direction of somebody you think you want, a coping mechanism.

Let me pause and say most strong Christians will find a way to help navigate seasons of neglect. Most strong Christians will find ways to deal with emotional, psychological, and verbal abuse. But life can become almost unbearable when you are dealing with neglect and abuse at the exact same time and for long periods of time. I should add that under no circumstances do I recommend a Christian—male or female—to tolerate or attempt to normalize physical abuse. It goes against all that is Godly and has no place in the Christian faith.

Concerning neglect: Your refusal to meet the God-ordained mental, spiritual, or physical needs of your spouse if they've been begging you for it, whatever it is, for seven years and now they don't beg for it anymore. It's not because they don't want it. They just don't want it from you. What has occurred is their body may be there with you, but their mind is on the other side of town. Sometimes coping mechanisms "wear jeans." What you used to do that you stopped doing, they're tempted to find somebody else who will do it. You're walking around with your chest stuck out like you were Mr. or Mrs. big stuff because you've been fighting all these years and all of a sudden, you think you've won. What you've been refusing to give they no longer ask for and you think you have won something when the truth is, you lost it. I want to warn married people that if there's something your spouse is begging you to deal with, deal with it before it's too late.

So I've shown you, first of all, that when it comes to wine running out, it is possible. I say that even for the one who was doing the asking, recognize that you may be coming closer to a point of no return than you think you are. It is possible. Let me push a little step further. Not only is it possible, but sometimes it's preventable.

In verses 1-3 of John chapter 2 as this wedding celebration was unfolding, near the end of the celebration on probably day six or day seven, they were almost out of wine. When you read the entirety of this collection of verses, the groom didn't know they were out of wine. The bride didn't know they were out of wine. The head waiter didn't know they were out of wine, which means the wedding coordinator didn't know that the wine had run out. Only the servants knew and the servants went to a family member and said to the family member, "We are about to run out of wine."

Why did they go to Mary? They didn't know anything about Mary being the mother of Jesus. They didn't know anything about Jesus's miracle-working power. They went to Mary because they knew as a family member, she would be concerned and do whatever she could to fix whatever was wrong, which put something in my spirit concerning your wine running out. My wine running out. It is this: Maybe you should have involved the right people sooner. I'm going to mess with you because if you've been where I've been, a startling reality hit me in separation, which led to the divorce. What hit me was all the people that I felt obligated to inform immediately after I announced to our church that our marriage was in trouble.

Let me see if I can put it better. Don't raise your hand but if you've gone through divorce, there was somebody you told "after" that you did not tell "before." Let me push it a little further. While you were going through trouble in the relationship, there were probably some people you talked to about it. They just couldn't do anything about it. So the question becomes, what if you had talked to the right people sooner? And why did you tell certain people "after the fact" but you didn't tell them before?

I called or wrote a specific list of people when my separation became public because I didn't want them to find out in the street. I wanted them to hear it from me. There was a list of people I wrote, and one by one I contacted them because I didn't want them to hear in the street what had occurred. I wanted them to hear it from me and the question I now ask myself is why did I call on the people on that list? Where did that list come from? That list was a list of people whose respect I had earned and whose love had made an impact on me. Here's what I now wrestle with: What if five years before I had called on them and they pulled me and my former wife into the same room, put one hand on her and one hand on me and helped pray and push us through what we had found ourselves in?

Maybe you should have involved the right people sooner because I want to warn you ma'am or sir. If you've been talking to the same person, your girlfriend, your cousin, whoever it is in your life, about the trouble you're having with your marriage. If all they do is "prop you up" and say things like, "You know what, you're right, they're wrong." If that's all they do, if they don't ever say, "Listen, can I bring the two of you together and we work this out now while there's still life in it?" Whoever that person is in your life that you've been going to, telling them about your problems and truth is, they love you and they mean well. They just aren't the right people. If that thing is on life support, find you somebody who can help put some life back into it before it's too late.

The overarching theme of John chapter 2 is that the servants (who were closest to the problem
and had the most to lose if the problem became public) took their problem to the person they felt was best suited to do something about it. Mary was obviously not wealthy, but it also must have been obvious to the servants that she cared deeply for her relative, the groom, until she would stop at nothing to try and make things right. So, it is possible. to run out of wine but it is sometimes preventable.

Here's the last thing I'd like to share, it is recoverable, which means even though your last water didn't turn into wine, your next water can turn into wine. Divorce is not a death sentence. God will let you love again. Now, take your time. Everything that glitters ain't gold. Take your time. Let God speak to you. Let God speak to them. Don't be in such a hurry. It is recoverable. Why?

Because Jesus can still turn water into wine.

Let me give you some advice and I'm done. If you've gone through divorce, here's the first thing I want to recommend that you do. Keep Jesus at the party. Don't go through all of that hellaciousness and then turn around and start walking in the flesh and pick up some new hellaciousness. Keep Jesus at the party. Keep him close by so that when Mr. or Mrs. Right show up, Jesus can point them out to you. Not your friend because you've got to watch some of them. "Girl, I think he's the one." You don't know anything about that man, ma'am! Or guys will hear things like, "Man, you'd better hold that one down." Truth is friend, you know about them but you don't truly know them. You need to let Jesus show you some things so you don't make new mistakes or remake the same mistakes you made previously. Keep Jesus at the party.

Here's the second one. Be willing to think outside of the box because the Lord may not work the way you think He's going to work. See, you keep going through your list of classmates. You're on Christiansmingle.com if there is such a thing. You are trying to search Instagram and Facebook. Can I tell you something about social media? Those people are not necessarily what their profile picture depicts. You know how I know this? If you're on social media and I go through your phone, I will see the 20 pictures you took in the same outfit until you found one out of the 20 you could work with. You added some filters and then uploaded it so that that "version of you" that we're seeing isn't the real you. Photoshop is something else. You've got to be willing to think outside of the box.

This past week I read a book by a dear colleague, Pastor Clinton McFarland, who also went through separation and divorce. He pastors a large church in Atlanta, Georgia and he preaches all over the country. He talked about how heartbroken he was that his marriage had died. He went into a deep state of depression and the Lord was able to pull him out. But one day he was at a Baptist convention and saw two ladies coming down a flight of stairs. In his book, he writes, the Lord said to him, "That's your wife."

He made an attempt to speak to her and she shut him down. He tried again the next day. She shut him down. He said, "Lord, did you really say what I thought you said?" but he didn't give up. He kept on pursuing her and ultimately tracked her down. She lived in a completely different state. She wasn't easy to get either. They're married today and he's as happy as he's ever been because he recognized that sometimes the Lord moves in mysterious ways. Think outside of the box.

Here's the last thing and I'm done. Number one: Keep Jesus at the party. Number two: Be willing to think outside of the box. And finally: Keep your pots clean and some water close by. Don't throw your pot away. Don't throw the water away. Keep the pots clean. Keep some water close by because Jesus can still turn water into wine.

PILLAR 2

Marriage is beautiful and can be an amazing blessing, but it can also be ugly and brutal if you do not have the right tools to deal with the bumps in the road.

Pastor Thorpe

My Story

THE FIRST TIME I ever saw or understood the concept of a relationship was when I observed my mom and dad, especially my mom.

One of the things she sought to teach me, and my other brothers daily, was how to treat a woman by not placing any undue burden on her and how to pick up after myself. She trained me in chivalry, which I practiced with any person I "courted." It's in my core foundation. I've always felt it was my responsibility to be a net positive in a woman's life, not someone who comes in and drains her. It's a partnership. Just like in business, there needs to be some equilibrium between the parties. If the man or the woman isn't happy, you may not have the best equilibrium.

When I looked at my dad, he was a great provider and an absolutely wonderful and supportive man. He got up every day, went to work, and ensured my mom and his children were well cared for. There was always food on the table. My siblings and I never had to leave our rooms and wonder if we would eat that day.

My home environment was not overly affectionate though. I always saw that as a gap I wanted to fill in my relationships. It was that constant examination of what I would do if I were married and how I would show love and affection to my family. Very early on, those were crucial observations that shaped how I viewed life and envisioned future relationships.

As I aged, my parents continued to instill those same values in me, such as a solid work ethic. They made being an adult and taking on responsibilities appealing. I was always impressed by how my mom never worked outside the home throughout my childhood. My dad earned enough to take care of the household, so that was the framework I had in life. I knew I needed a good job early because if I were going to be married, I would have to live up to those responsibilities. I consequently completed training in a career as a diesel mechanic early on and then, by the age of 20, I was married.

The story of how I got married goes as follows: We were high school sweethearts, dating since we were 14. We both came from a traditional household, but hers was filled with some challenges that caused her to see life through a much different lens. Things were not as easy and carefree as they were for me. At some point, maybe she will write her own book and explain how things were for her growing up. For now, it is not my story to tell but I will say this, adversity as a child must be addressed at some point or it will hinder your future successes. We both graduated early at 17, and we parted ways for a short time but reconnected later on. By Christmas of our 19th year, we were engaged and by 20, we were married.

Looking back, I now believe that we were simply too young and lacked a lot of experience and "real world" exposure as it relates to relationships. This is not the only reason our marriage didn't work out but it was a major contributing factor. I was constantly trying to fix things that I had not broken, heal things that I had not hurt, and fill voids that only God could fill. In my mind, I was totally up for the challenge. In hindsight, I now see that I became part of the problem. I was attempting to always fix things that only she and God could fix together. Neither of us had really dated anyone else and perhaps our perspective had not been broadened enough to reveal more of what life had to offer and what it would take to really make things work. We deeply admired and respected each other, which allowed us to last as long as we did through our school years. The attributes that enable people to make it through school relationships are not, however, the same attributes necessary for two people to have a robust and lasting marriage.

We didn't have anyone around us to tell us not to marry young or to caution us to slow things down. Personally, I may have appeared to people to be mature for my age, and they may have thought I was mature enough to make that major life decision, so no one ever cautioned us that we were too young or that marriage was not the right thing to be doing. I think they all thought we were competent enough to make that decision.

Looking back, I do not know if that was the right way of thinking or the correct position for others. I appreciated the freedom we were given and, in some ways, earned by demonstrating a good head on our shoulders, but we were still kids. Maybe if someone had taken the time to explain to us why we should not get married, we could have changed course, but that did not happen.

We married in 1993 and at the time, I was an associate minister in my home church. As she had been around the church, I was confident that she understood ministry and what that type of job entailed.

In 1998, I was asked to be the pastor of Faith Church. That's when we started commuting from Jacksonville,

Florida, to Gainesville, which is 72 miles one way. We made that trek at least twice a week—at times seven days a week—and we both still worked full-time jobs. This commuting lasted for three-and-a-half years. This was an important period which causes me to pause now and issue a major word of caution. Compatibility is important and it comes with rules that I shared earlier and will expand on later. In some ways, serving a church as a pastor has received some negative and unfair criticism. Can it be demanding? Absolutely. Consuming? You had better believe it. But for the person who's been called to it, ministering as a pastor can also be incredibly rewarding. Being able to read the scripture and see men and women who sacrificed much for the causes of God transforms those people from biblical personalities into heroes and standard-setters. Here is the revelation though that I must share: These same characteristics are present in EACH and EVERY "career" that someone pursues. Doctors, nurses, attorneys, educators and administrators can all become immersed in what it is that they have been called to do.

Here is a false assumption: "I need to be married to someone who appreciates and supports what I have been called to do." NO! What you really need is someone who has their own calling and life and can IDENTIFY with your struggles because in many ways, they share them. Later I will discuss three personality types: Career people, Job people, and Dreamers. It's going to be important to identify which category you fall into and to select a spouse that falls into the same category. I actually used to think that once we started having children that this would create an environment that would give her many things for her to pour herself into. God saw otherwise. Because of circumstances that neither of us could control or cause, having children would not be in our future.

For the early years of marriage, everything was going well. It was the early stage of us loving each other and enjoying marriage. We had even built our first home by the age of 24. It was the same year I was called and began commuting to Faith Church. We both had solid full-time jobs in our home town and personally, I was doing something that I had dreamed of for a decade, becoming a full-time senior pastor. On top of that, I had led the church through multiple lucrative real estate transactions and we had constructed a brand-new church building. A major change occurred in 2001. Our church constructed a new building and moved to a new location. For the first time, I was becoming a new full-time senior pastor. This also meant that we would sell our new house in Jacksonville and relocate to Gainesville.

By 2002 an even more drastic change occurred, and we could never recover fully. In that year, the church was beginning to grow as people from all across the country who had moved into the Gainesville area came to see our services, primarily due to our robust television ministry. At one time, we aired more than 20 times each week and on multiple channels. For me, it was the answer to my prayers and a career-long goal to be the full-time senior pastor of a growing and vibrant church. For her though, I believe it was the opposite. She was away from our home town and our families for the first time and working on a new job. Perhaps it was the fear of the unknown that gripped her the tightest. Life in a new environment and seeing me excited about new people we were both meeting for the first time. Being unsure of what everyone's motives were and whether or not I, as her husband, would be able to spot ill motives all proved to be more than we could handle. By 2002, it was apparent that we were in over our heads. It is not that either of us were bad people, but we were different people and those differences were about to drive us apart.

I always believed that things could work out so long as the two people were willing to see it through and try to make it work. At the time, I thought that with a little time and effort, we could rekindle and maintain the love, trust, and devotion of the first initial years. As time dragged on, that was becoming increasingly unlikely.

The Lesson

MARRIAGE IS HARD, and I had a romanticized view going into it. Marriage is beautiful and can be an amazing blessing, but it can also be ugly and brutal if you do not have the right tools to deal with the bumps in the road. The lesson in this story is to understand what you are getting into. Understand the other person and what is expected of you within the relationship. Every relationship is unique and will require different things to ensure it lasts. Take the time to look into those things to ensure you are both on the same page.

Also, pay attention to the red flags displayed for you. I think I always knew the type of person she was and the kind of person I was, but I chose to ignore any concerns. My life was going through incredible changes rapidly, and I did not have the bandwidth to look deeply enough into her issues. It was only when an argument would occur that the problems arose for me. But you need to pay attention to things in your relationship and take the proper steps to make sure you either can remedy them or accept that maybe you made a mistake and it's time to move on with your life separately. For me, I had reached this painful place by 2005 when I first contacted an attorney about divorce. Keep in mind, this was after I begged and pleaded that we seek and get counseling from anyone she would feel comfortable with. She insisted that we did not need it. I still stayed and tried for another eight tumultuous years.

I pray for you, if you're still unmarried, that you will discover differences in your dating phases. Ask tough questions and be honest with each other about what the answers are. When you choose to ignore them or live with a fairy-tale mentality of what marriage is, you are setting yourself up for heartbreak once those realities come slapping you in the face.

The Revelation

LOOKING BACK, I can now examine where things went wrong and contemplate how things could have been done better. In my current professional life, which often involves counseling, I am not the person who will tell someone they should not get married, but I will tell someone they are not ready to get married. My ex-wife and I gave the impression to the people around us that we were intelligent, well-rounded people who had it all figured out when we got engaged at 19. It seemed we did not need to be monitored because if we were getting married, we knew what we were doing. In reality, we did not know what we were doing. Honestly, it's easy to look back and say this in hindsight, but I genuinely believe we should not have gotten married or at the very least, waited a little longer to learn more about each other and contemplate if we were right for each other. I think we both wanted to get married but at that age, we did not understand the complex realities of marriage.

When you are that young, I also think you do not spend enough time asking the right questions to ensure you two are on the same page in all parts of your life. We never went over how we viewed intimacy within the confines of a relationship. A lack of affection may be okay when you're a teenager and may not be a significant concern. But devotion and love are sometimes needed to make it through the day as your career excels and goes into new dimensions. If I had known more about these things when I was 19, it would have prepared me better for my late 20s and early 30s as I began to appreciate more how the physical aspect of the relationship needs to be in sync.

This is not to say I did not love my first wife or that we did not try everything possible to make it work. But when your struggles begin to come from multiple directions all at once, it can reach the point where even when you are the Godliest of people, you begin to contemplate things that were never on the table. I grew up watching my parents and how they were but naively, I looked at it from an outside perspective. I did not know what was happening behind closed doors because they did not show me those things or discuss with me aspects of the intimate physical relationship.

AFFIRMATION

It's not foolish to be in love.

It's foolish to believe love is all you need for a healthy, lifelong relationship.

PILLAR 3

Even if you are not stressed in your marriage, it is essential to find something that keeps you busy and focused.

Pastor Thorpe

My Story

THE STRESS FROM ALL THE YEARS of struggle I was experiencing, both in my marriage and the responsibilities of my career, was taking a toll on my health. We had completed one successful building project, and I was being asked by another agency to build a large addition onto our new church to serve as a community and neighborhood fitness center complete with fully staffed after-school and summer programs. Midway through the planning phase, the other nonprofit began to backpedal, which left me a bit rattled. I went to the doctor, who recommended that I deal with the stress by finding something fun to pour some of my energy into and keep me sane. So around 2004, I began looking into ways to destress.

I made an assessment of everything I was facing, especially workwise, and made a list of all the things that were adding to my discomfort. I made a separate list of my most engaged volunteers and staff members, and I did something revolutionary. I started delegating all the stressful things to the team members I thought were best suited to tackle them on an ongoing basis. This was liberating.

Removing stressors is one thing, but finding fun is something else. For me, something I inherited from my parents was looking sharp and dressing your best. I started giving some consideration to starting a suit business. I had always liked suits and how they convey an image of professionalism. My beloved pastor, the late Rev. Dr. David A Lattimore Jr, believed and taught that senior pastors should always be in a suit and tie during business hours. I had been a busy person being a pastor, but this was a side gig that let me escape from some of the realities of my work and home life. This was not a substitute for facing reality, but it was a healthy outlet that allowed me to pour parts of myself into something both fun and rewarding.

There was a particular brand of suit that my pastor and I liked wearing. He and I were buying so many that I wanted to buy them wholesale instead of retail, so I contacted the suit company and inquired about buying my suits directly from them. They said they could sell suits to me at wholesale prices if I got a business license. I did but they reneged and wouldn't sell to me initially because I wasn't in a brick-and-mortar store. I had to do some finagling, so it took two months before they gave me a contract.

Business people can be very ruthless at times, but coming from a pastoral background helped me remain patient and show respect to those I was working with. I think showing someone respect so they know they can work with you goes a long way when dealing with business people.

In the meantime, the store manager in Orlando where I was originally buying my suits said, "Pastor Thorpe, you can take anything out of our store, and we will mark it up by $40 from the wholesale price. You can sell it to your friends at whatever price you want." So that's what I did. Then I realized that one of the brands I was selling through my partnership with the Orlando store had a website and a link to the designer on the brand's website. I contacted the designer who suggested I could sell custom suits and recommended I do it through him.

Selling suits is one thing, but selling custom suits is a good business because everyone wants something that resonates with them. The designer was willing to work with me, which was the perfect situation.

He and I had a great working relationship that lasted for several years. We had a good

friendship outside of business but with one flaw. He told me the suits were being produced in

Italy, and that's why his prices were so high. I believed him without question but one day, after receiving some suits from him, I realized there was paperwork accidentally left in one of the pockets with a number on it. I saw it was in an Asian language, so I took it to a Chinese restaurant out of sheer curiosity. They told me it was Korean. I knew a Korean coffee shop, so I took it there. They showed me how to dial the numbers, which I did when I got home, and a guy answered.

I told him about the clients I funneled through the designer, and he told me he made the suits. Having that knowledge, I questioned why I had to work through the original guy when I could just work with the man making the suits. I asked if I could deal with him directly, and he liked the idea.

This arrangement was a boom to my business because I could drop the prices that day. Initially, I was charging $1,000 for a two-piece suit. The price went down to $600. A three-piece suit went from $1,200 to $750. I do not think the other guy was scamming me. The mark-up was just the nature of the business. He was the designer who then had someone else make the suit. With it being a custom suit venture, I did not need a designer because the customers already told me what they wanted the suit to look like.

When the opportunity to work with the actual people making the suit came about, it was a good business decision on my part. Of course, it was by good fortune that the ticket was in the suit pocket.

I continue to work in the suit business to this day, even though I have had adventures in that sector. It helped to create a healthy outlet from some of the marital struggles and add some fun to things. It did not get rid of them.

The Lesson

I DON'T NEED TO REMIND MOST PEOPLE, but stress kills. Stress can come from many different areas, not just marriage. I think I have slightly grayer hair thanks to my past marriage than I would otherwise have. Even if you are not stressed in your marriage, it is essential to find something fun that keeps you busy, focused, and calm. It has to be something you want to do. Being a pastor was my main thing, but even being a pastor can be stressful—rewarding, but also stressful. I needed to find something else. I liked suits, so I went into the suit business. The objective was not to keep the lights on because I was not trying to get wealthy from selling suits. I just wanted something to occupy my time and take my attention away from the pain I was feeling at home. The suit business could do that for me. I could distract myself from all the other things in my life and just do and deal with things I liked, such as suits. I think that is the key for anyone going through something stressful.

Opening a business can be stressful because you have to deal with an extra set of things, but this situation was unique because money was not my goal. I was doing okay then financially. Whatever I made from the business was supplemental income. I was not trying to compete with the high-end suit firms of the world. I was just trying to maintain my minor operation. Once the stress of money was taken away, things turned out better. It would have been a different outcome if I had needed the money from the business to put food on the table. This is also a key to picking something that will not stress your life. If you like fish, sell it, but do not get into it because you need money to keep the lights on. You need to pick something that has no real significance in your life other than you simply like doing it. I've since become very successful at doing this. I've worked with more than 20 factories around the world and I have developed an impressive client base, many of whom are now my personal friends and some of my professional heroes and heroines.

The Revelation

I DO THINK THIS WAS THE TIME when I started to realize that my ex-wife and I were not going to work out. The business was beginning to relieve the stress from my life, but I think it also revealed to me the origins of that stress. When you do something that brings you a little bit of joy and then have to walk into a house filled with arguing and confrontation, it opens your eyes more to what is going on in your life. The business was the best thing to help me understand my situation. It may have even helped speed up the divorce process because I could see the stark contrast in my life. I began to question why I was still in a failing relationship. It helped me open my eyes and maybe even move on in my mind faster.

It also showed my entrepreneurial side. I had never run my own business and even though it was very low-level, it showed me that I could do something outside of ministry. Pastoring is always going to be in my life, but if for some reason things do not work out in that department, at least I know I am capable of running a business. But I don't think I could ever be one of those money-hungry people. If I opened another business, it would be for the enjoyment of having such a venture and selling what I like, not simply to make tons of money. I was blessed to develop another skill that could last me a long time when I opened a business.

AFFIRMATION

Healthy ventures outside of a relationship help clear minds, which makes for sound decision-making.

PILLAR 4

I assumed my business would be all over the town, but it wasn't.

Pastor Thorpe

My Story

BY 2013, my ex-wife and I had had many talks about separation. Let me reiterate that God absolutely hates divorce, and I do too. God considers it a "violent dismembering" of what was designed to last forever. I have devoted most of my adult life now to preparing people for marriage by encouraging them to be selective when they date and keep sex out of the equation because it can cloud your judgment and ruin your chances of finding your true person. Ultimately, I did not leave our marital home voluntarily, I was asked to leave. After nearly 20 years of marriage and 11 years of battling, I acquiesced and I left.

She asked that I not make our separation public and I did not. My only stipulation was that if a rumor or talk ever surfaced, I would announce it to our church immediately.

Not too long after my ex-wife and I separated, I was approached to run for the county commission. I told the organizers that I was not in a position at the time but I would get back to them at some point in the future. My fear was always that if my separation became public, it would shatter any public image that I had and politics would be off the table. It was not until I made the announcement to our church that my former wife and I were separated that I communicated with the organizers who were asking me to consider running for office. I didn't think they would want to work with someone who was separated. I imagined that wouldn't look good on the campaign trail and maybe the opponent would try to exploit that flaw about me. So I called the individuals encouraging me to be a candidate to inform them of the separation and how I felt I would not be a worthy candidate.

They responded, "Don't let that be the reason," and confirmed that they thought I would be an excellent commissioner. I consequently ended up running for office most of the time that elapsed from my separation to the finalization of the divorce.

That actually turned out to be very helpful for me because it allowed me to pour into my community instead of thinking about all of the pain I was experiencing, which was obviously still weighing heavy on my shoulders. I must share this: Being separated for a year could have been an opportunity for the two of us to self-reflect, make adjustments, and try again. I sincerely wished that could have been the case but it was not. That year was spent rehashing what caused us to separate in the first place. I felt this was incredibly counterproductive, but I was only one part of the equation and I could not control what anyone else did. We actually made more progress after the divorce was final as it relates to understanding how things that occurred during childhood had played a dangerous role in adult life and marriage. Apologies were offered and accepted.

Once the political campaign kicked off, I immersed parts of myself in it. I was campaigning roughly 14 hours daily, which takes a lot out of you. What made my campaign unique was that I was recruited by some people who I later found out didn't necessarily get along. This created problems when it came to organizing a cohesive campaign and finances. I had all the responsibility to raise money for the campaign. I spent a lot of my own money to keep the ship moving.

Throughout the time I was working to win the election, I still had to deal with calls from my ex-wife every day or every other day. She wanted me to listen to her position about the separation and why we fell into our broken cycle.

In her opinion, I was ruining the marriage by leaving in the first place. So while I was out there shaking hands and kissing babies, I had to deal with our stressful interactions.

The election primaries were over in August, with the general election in November. It was a struggle, and I did not know how the winds would turn, but I did my best and was neutral about the outcome. I wanted to win, but I still had the pain of my broken relationship on my mind. Being separated was difficult because I enjoyed marriage, and I consequently still held out some hope for reconciliation.

The Lesson

WHEN SOMETHING IS COMPLETED it is the rebirth of something else. As our marriage ended, I was immersing myself in politics. God opened a new door for me as He closed another. Grief shows up in many different ways. I thought that it would be depression and sadness. Although those emotions were churning on the inside because my marriage failed, neither was apparent from my outward appearance. God didn't allow me to stop what He was doing in my life. The same things I tried to turn away from, He brought toward me. The more we held on, the further we fell apart. Only when we fully separated could we see clearly that our paths were set in another direction. You can't have a testimony without a test. As much as I honored marriage, I didn't want others hurt because of my life. God used my first marriage to help not only me and my ex to move on but so that other couples could realize God's love is not based on our emotions or failings. It wasn't the end of the world when I left, it was the beginning of my deeper understanding of who God is and how much He loves us.

This was a hard road to travel, and I don't endorse divorce, but it happened to me. You are ending a covenant. There are a lot of emotions that you go through, and you have to have the right people around you. You want to make sure that there is no resolution before taking that step. Counseling and all those other measures are put in place to help, but sometimes it is just over. When it is known that God still loves you and He wants better for you and the other person involved, you can move forward with peace and confidence.

The Revelation

I WAS MORE BROKEN on the inside than I let on. I wasn't even willing to acknowledge to myself the level of pain I was experiencing. Being a pastor and simply being the type of person I am, I always try to keep that face on. You want the people in your congregation and life to not worry about you. I was truly broken on the inside. I never imagined the end of my marriage despite the fact that during the separation, the writing was clearly on the wall.

I took as a sign of my failure the fact nothing was going well in my own home. If I could not hold on to my marriage, then what could I hold on to? It was like the trauma that led to my separation led me to judge all of my life and feel like I would be viewed as a fraud and a failure. I spoke so much about relationships as a pastor, yet my own marriage was failing..

I don't think I was ever really able to process what was happening because I had to always keep a smile on my face to not worry anybody and because I was campaigning. In hindsight, I wish I had given myself more time to mourn.

AFFIRMATION

People are a lot more understanding than you think.

PILLAR 5

Everything you've heard me say about marriage and family is true, and I stand behind it 100 percent.

Pastor Thorpe

My Story

THE DAY THE DIVORCE WAS FINALIZED, we drove to Union County. She didn't want to be there because she still did not want to go through with the divorce. All mediation had failed, so we let the judge decide the terms of the divorce.

By then, the only thing on my mind was survival. I had no long-term plans. I was thinking mainly about how I would handle things financially going forward. During the 10 months of separation, I paid nearly all of the expenses for both households.

Thankfully, along with my regular salary, the suit business helped to sustain things. I knew this could not continue beyond the divorce being final because spousal support payments could also be involved. Each state has different laws concerning alimony or spousal support. In Florida, it is calculated based on the length of the marriage and the difference between the income of both parties. For me, this felt unfair morally. It felt as though I was being penalized by the courts for fighting so long to try to make things work. Current laws in Florida have changed that so now, retroactively, they make more sense for both parties. After setting the spousal support amount and a brief discussion on the division of property, assets, and liabilities, the judge concluded the proceedings. In less than 30 minutes, what had lasted nearly 21 years legally came to an abrupt end. Mentally and physically, I felt no different at all, which was very surprising to me. I didn't feel compelled to tell anyone or make it known in any way. It was months later before I made the church aware, and even longer before I informed my immediate family. Informing people of the initial separation, I guess, was traumatic enough.

The separation announcement occurred in the middle of 2013 and the divorce was final near the end of 2014. As I reflect on it now, the truth is that I hated talking about it and kind of wished it would all just go away. For most people who get a divorce, their main worry is how the family will react. For a pastor, it's different. I have a congregation that looks to me for guidance. It was already a struggle to tell them we were separated. Once we were divorced, I shuddered when wondering what their reaction would be.

The Lesson

EVEN THOUGH my first marriage did not work out, my convictions were strong. They're even stronger now around the idea of marriage. I understood a prescription for a successful marriage, but unfortunately, that was not what I had.

I remember telling some younger members on the day I announced that I was separated that everything you've heard me say about marriage and family is true, and I stand behind it 100 percent. I didn't want them to think I was preaching one thing and living something else. That wasn't the case. I tried to live what I preached. I have helped so many couples through my ministry. Years ago, long before my separation, I visited a local bank. The manager said, "Pastor Thorpe, the word on the street is if someone wants to save their marriage, then they should go to Pastor Thorpe's church." It was just something I talked about so much.

The lesson is not to avoid getting married but to approach marriage the right way. Ask the right questions and get to know the person you are preparing to spend the rest of your life with. Do not get caught up in the feelings and emotions in those first couple of months together. When you meet someone and have that initial connection, it will feel like a burst of emotion that you will correlate to love.

I cannot tell you if you are in love, only you know the answer. What I am saying is do not rush into things. You are potentially going to have 50 or 60 years with this one person. What is the rush? The lessons from my previous marriage must be for others to heed. Make sure you and that person connect in ways that can guarantee a long, healthy marriage. It is all about finding yourself, finding another person, understanding if you two have things in common, and then looking to build from there. Marriage should not be on the table until you both are sure you are on the same page.

The Revelation

I LOVED MY EX-WIFE, and she loved me, but we were not meant to be together. Maybe if we had done more to get to know each other, then our divorce would not have happened, but we unfortunately cannot change the past. Sometimes I ask myself if there was more I could have done or if there was more we as a couple could have done to make the marriage work. But I look back, and I do not think so. I think we exhausted all of the options we had. We did our best to overcome some of the issues, but in the end, they were too monumental.

That makes me realize I should not be sad or happy that my marriage ended. I must be realistic and ambivalent because ending a marriage is never good. When you get married, you want to be together for the rest of your life, but that is not how things always end. Knowing that I did everything I could to try and make it work helps me sleep easily at night instead of thinking about that one option I left on the table.

AFFIRMATION

The hardest thing to do is end something but sometimes, it is the only thing you can do.

PILLAR 6

I have always understood the expectations placed upon pastors.

Pastor Thorpe

My Story

IN 2019, I was asked to consider the senior pastor position for a church in Jacksonville, Florida. Actually, it was two churches at the same time. This situation is always delicate when you are already serving a loving and supportive congregation. Pastors must be open to the idea and sensitive to God's plan to move them in different seasons so even though I had never considered leaving my church before this option arose, I thought it would be a good opportunity for some very specific reasons. Both of my parents were requiring more of my attention as they aged and their health situations were changing. I was open to the idea of moving back and serving a church in my hometown, which would put me closer to my parents who lived there.

I agreed to an interview with one of the churches, which was typical except for one question they had asked me in a written questionnaire about what duties I thought fell to the pastor's wife. That caught me a little off guard, and I replied that the pastor's wife doesn't owe the church anything because she is not their employee. A wife can have a good role in the church, but just because a woman is married to a pastor does not automatically mean she has to be intricately involved in the church.

Prior to the in-person interview, Individuals involved in the search contacted me and said they thought I had misled them, which baffled me. They made the assumption I was married even though they had been to my Gainesville church and by that point, it was widely known I was divorced. If they had asked me, I would have told them I was divorced. Even my resume made no mention of being married or having a wife.

Once they found out about my divorce, they wanted to reschedule my in-person visit. By that time, I had decided that I wasn't going back. I could see that being divorced was going to be a problem with them, so I knew it was best if I kept away from the situation. It was only thanks to one of my ministry mentors, Bishop Rudolph Mckissick Sr., who at age 94 said I should go back, that I ended up scheduling the second conversation.

When I arrived for the interview, they sent me to meet the deacons. There were about 18 men, all over age 65. To start, they wanted everyone to introduce themselves. The deacons started and they each made it a point to mention they were married and how long they had each been with their spouse. Once they did that, I said, "Okay, I see where this is going." I thought they should have been ashamed of themselves. I have been around a while, so I know that longevity doesn't mean success. Stating how long a couple has been married does not mean either spouse is happy in the relationship, but I didn't go there.

I didn't get the job. The preacher they hired quit after 12 months, and he got married only a few months before they called him to be their pastor. In the end, I did not want to be part of something that would pressure me to get married. I knew God would bring me a life partner whenever I was meant to find one. Make no mistake about it—I was ready to find her.

The Lesson

PEOPLE WILL WANT you to be a certain way to meet their expectations, but you can only be yourself. I did not like the fact that I was divorced, but I was not hiding it. I was not afraid to talk about it. I certainly was not going to rush into something serious with another person for a job at that time.

You need to be true to yourself and recognize that your story is yours. No one can take that away from you. People will want to judge you, but those people do not understand you or your story. I could have explained to those deacons what I had been through in my life, and it would not have mattered. They were simply interested in the image of me being married because, in their eyes, that was the image a pastor was supposed to portray.

To an extent, I understand where they were coming from, but marriage was not my reality at that time. I was not going to hide that fact. You likewise should not hide your truth. Whatever you are going through, having it in the open will feel better than hiding it. Some people may judge you, but then you know those people are not the people you want in your life. People want to pretend they know what is best for you, but only you decide what you need in your life. I hid my divorce for a while, but once I got it out to the world, I was no longer running from my story. I was not announcing it on the loudspeaker at the local football game, but people knew my truth.

I wanted people to understand but realized my desire was not realistic and should not be seen as mandatory. If people did not like that I was divorced, then there was nothing I could do about it. When you are in a situation or have gone through an experience that people cannot understand, just brush it off and keep moving.

The Revelation

I HAVE ALWAYS UNDERSTOOD the expectations placed upon pastors. Even so, it hurts to feel like you are not good at your job simply because you do not meet preconceived expectations. I know pastors who may be dating someone but are not yet married. I do not think there is anything different about the way they preach, and they do not allow their marital status to influence how they approach their congregation.

Being judged by fellow church folks for not being married really did hurt. It was like I was being looked down upon for making the decision I thought was best for me. But it was a good opportunity to learn that there are some people who do not have your best interest at heart. Some people just want you to fit a mold and never change.

The irony was that as I was being judged for not having a spouse, it was my heart's desire and sincere prayer that God would allow me to find my true soulmate.

AFFIRMATION

Nobody knows what is best for your life but you.

PILLAR 7

I also believe God will not do things for you that you can do yourself.

You have to be able to make hard decisions for the betterment of everyone involved.

Pastor Thorpe

My Story

AFTER THE DIVORCE WAS FINALIZED, I could have been the person who hated love and thought there was no hope of me finding love again. While there was a little bit of fear of going through the heartache I had just endured with another woman, in the end, singleness was not my character.

I love love, and I would not give up on finding it. What may surprise some is that I dated three different women while single, and they were relatively long-term relationships. But I didn't go looking for them. They found me.

The first lady I dated was a mother of four wonderful children. While we did grow close, I was not considering marriage during the early stages of our relationship, in part because I knew I would be asking my family and church members to embrace not only her but her children.

In and of itself this was not a problem, but dating her made me become aware of the fact my family and that of my ex-wife were intertwined, which would likely be a complication with anyone I dated. My ex-wife and I had known each other since we were 14, which created a strong bond between our relatives. Even now, both families gather when a loved one passes. I recognized that anyone who came into my life would have to put up with that family dynamic, which is not easy.

I was also hesitant to consider pursuing a marriage commitment because she developed significant financial issues. I am never against helping someone and especially a person I am in a relationship with, so I didn't have a problem supporting her. My concern was that I was still not feeling stable financially after the divorce, so there was a strain in our relationship. It did not take long for me to realize the timing was all wrong. The divorce was still clearly in the rearview mirror, making it far too soon to pursue a serious relationship.

The second relationship kind of piggybacked off the first one. The young lady was a single mom who had been married, and she carried this facade of financial stability and affluence. Part of my thinking was that I wouldn't have the stress in this relationship like the last one because she gave the appearance of someone good with money, so I went for it.

This relationship exposed me to some unique things I had not seen before. For example, I was not used to an adolescent child attending a fine dining restaurant and ordering whatever they wanted off the menu. Not everyone grew up like me, so I tried to roll with it and see where I fit in but soon realized the extent of her money problems.

It became obvious that we had very different perspectives about more than how children should be raised. This truth was cemented when we talked about marriage and decided to look at rings. I took her to one of the stores where I had bought jewelry for years. While browsing their inventory and catalog, she was not impressed. We went to a different store where she chose a $31,000 ring. I knew at that moment that we had very different values, and she was probably not the right woman for me.

We'd had conversations about my wariness of the long-term prospects of this relationship, and I was set on ending the relationship. She responded that we didn't have to think about marriage. We could keep things as they were, and that was okay at the time, but then she started dropping hints about marriage again. I still did not want to marry her so once that happened, the relationship ended.

Doing so was difficult because there is something in me that doesn't want to hurt people at all. But I also believe God will not do things for you that you can do yourself, and you have to be able to make hard decisions for the betterment of everyone involved. There come seasons when you know your time is up where you are. You must trust God with the details of how you move forward. She was a great woman, just not the woman for me.

I dated another person some time later after breaking up with the second young lady. That third relationship was a significant learning experience, as the Lord taught me some stuff. The relationship came about when my dad was terminally ill in 2019. He passed away the same year, and that was probably the wrong time to get into a relationship. This taught me that there are times when it is not wise to pursue dating.

The other thing it taught me—and I say this as a spiritual term—is that everything that glitters spiritually is not gold. One of the things that attracted me to this young lady was that she taught classes on marriage and family at her church every Sunday morning. She had been married before and was also a preacher's kid, so I thought she would understand me and my world.

I was enthralled with this lady who graduated with her master's degree within three months of our dating. I bought her a diamond and sapphire Rolex watch as a graduation gift, but our relationship changed course before I gave it to her. What came off as the appearance of insecurity, and perhaps, inflexibility eventually made me realize she also was not the wife I was ultimately seeking.

I still had the suit business at that time. She was looking at my business Facebook page and noticed my cellphone number was used as part of an advertising campaign. She said she didn't think it was appropriate that I had my number as a part of my ads.

I said to myself, "Now, wait a minute. I have been in business since 2004. People have always had access to my cell phone number, which has never been a problem." At first, I didn't see the number as an issue, but I was like, "You know what, YOU see it as an issue, so I'll consider it." I went to the page and removed the number.

Later she suggested that I go through my Google calendar and remove any data that had anything to do with not just anyone I had ever known but all of their family members. We had a conversation about that, and she wanted me to delete the birth dates of my nieces and nephews.

She said she thought I may be tempted to see those dates and reach out to person I had been in a relationship with. This was within a week of the phone number incident. By that point, I had become better at recognizing red flags and calling them out in the moment.

I told her, "I'll tell you what I want to do. I want you to give me a week to pray about what you're asking me to do so I can determine if this is the direction I want my life to go in because this must be a part of who you are and how you view life and relationships."

She replied, "No, you cannot have a week. You must decide now because this issue is important." With the purest heart, I said, "You are not the person for me, and trying to go any further would be to your detriment and mine." That ended the relationship. The breakup beat me up for a while. I never find joy in breaking someone's heart or in having my own heart broken.

All of these relationships taught me a lesson. I learned the importance of not allowing relationships to be clouded by physical aspects. In dating, when you connect physically before other pieces fall into place, you are just stretching out something that is not good for you. It also taught me what I was not willing to put up with.

I also learned how to have boundaries around women and develop standards that I would take into any future relationship. I was determined not to make the same mistakes I made in these dating situations.

The Lesson

DATING WAS NOT EASY when I was coming up, and dating is still not easy. You do not go into the dating world thinking everything will be okay. Whether you are someone coming of age or someone who just finished a relationship, you need to be prepared to take the lumps that come with dating and try to learn from them. The most significant part is learning.

If you are going to date, you need to understand why problems occurred and what you can do to ensure they do not happen again. While dating the second woman, I began to understand what I wanted, which was to be married. I just needed to develop a game plan, which does not happen in a week or a month. It could take years and require being in any number of relationships. I still moved on to a third relationship without a clear roadmap, and that relationship also ended.

You need to take your time in the dating world. Do not rush into anything. Look at what is available to you from an emotional point of view. What I mean by that is do not let desire take over. Keep your head on right and look for the person who will make you feel good in the long run.

The Revelation

I THINK YOU CAN BE DILIGENT in wanting God's best. I completed a series entitled "My life is in your hands" dealing with the book of Ruth. There is so much in the first two chapters alone, as Naomi loses her husband and two sons amid a famine. She is not only heartbroken, but she has some anger issues and resentment issues toward God. That did not change her focus on seeing God's hand move, even during her period of grief and disappointment.

One of the things I shared with the congregation was that while you are grieving, you have to open yourself up for the Lord to give you insight and vision. That allows you to see things and to process what you see. You have to prepare for it going into grief because grief can be so consuming and overwhelming.

In the same fashion that you must be deliberate in making funeral arrangements, you also need to be intentional in a psychological sense and recognize that God can show you some things in grief that you cannot see when things are going well. The only way to embrace those things is to be deliberate in looking for them. People miss opportunities to recover and thrive because their eyes are closed while suffering.

That is something I had to learn after the breakups. I had to take some time to grieve, but I also needed to get back into the world because the worst type of suffering is when you are suffering in silence. You do not want to go through something in your house alone with the lights off. You need to get back out there. It was not easy at the moment and I definitely had to overcome self-doubt but in the end, if it was not for God sending me those messages and me catching them, I do not know where I would be.

AFFIRMATION

Putting yourself back out there is the best way to move on with your life.

PILLAR 8

I didn't have the desire to date.
I wanted to be married.

Pastor Thorpe

My Story

I NEED TO THANK each of the women I dated following my divorce. It was because of the time I spent with them that I was able to develop rules regarding dating. Because of the failed dating relationships, I was able to refine rigid standards that I would take into the next phase of my dating journey.

I was sure that I wanted a wife, but not just any wife. She would have to fit within my new standards. The first one was that I needed to trust her. The main way she would be able to acquire my trust was if she demonstrated maturity. I judge maturity differently than others. For me, maturity is based on the fruit of the Spirit. I needed to see someone who carried herself well, took pride in how she presented herself and had the same mentality I had regarding wanting to be married. I was not interested in playing any more games. I wanted someone focused on being married.

The second thing is that it needed to be someone I was compatible with. I defined that as meaning she would not embarrass me. It's a harsh word for me but it's a core word from a relationship perspective. I think when two people have two different values, that leads to embarrassment because at your core, you are who you are. If you marry someone opposite to who you are, the manifestation of that cannot only have a private impact but a public impact, and a lot of aspects of my life are very public.

The third requirement was that I needed someone I was physically attracted to, and that is very important for obvious reasons. I believe intimacy and affection are crucial in a relationship. Without them, I think all aspects of the relationship fall apart.

Over time, the Lord added a fourth caveat that caught me off guard: I needed to be with someone who was into me. At that stage of my life, I didn't have time to convince someone of my worth because it could take years for some people to figure it out. It would have to be someone who knew enough about me or had investigated me sufficiently that I was not trying to convince them of who I was.

I decided, "Lord, whoever the person is that you are going to give to me, they have to know I am

going to be in it, that they are going to be able to count on me, and that my heart will be a safe place for their heart." Honestly, I could not conceive where that woman would come from, but it was an absolute requirement that I would not expend my energy trying to convince someone that I was a good catch.

Once I developed these standards, I concluded that I would not get into another relationship if the requirements were not met because I didn't have the desire to date. I wanted to be married. I felt called to marriage but was not going to force a situation in which I was not 100% confident. I know what doesn't work for me and what I will not settle for. I was resolute in that thinking.

I was honest with myself in admitting I didn't know where the right relationship would come from, if that person existed, or if she could come into my life because those are some pretty rigid standards. But I trusted in God and, thankfully, He had the perfect woman waiting right under my nose.

The Lesson

I DO NOT BELIEVE there is anything wrong with having standards and choosing not to be in a relationship with just anyone. Some people may call it being picky, while others may call it being calculated. I was tired of going through the rotating doors of relationships. I needed to create standards and stick to them, which I think is the biggest lesson.

When you set standards for the people you will engage with romantically, you must adhere to them. We get lost in the moment, seeing a beautiful person across from us, and we lose ourselves. You need to bring yourself back into focus and remember why you made the list in the first place. You are not looking for short-term gratification. You are looking for something that looks long-term and healthy. If you want to be married, you must remember the rules you set that you believe will be the best way to find that person.

Keep your focus, and do not get distracted by the first thing that glitters. It can be hard, but remember that marriage is the goal. Just because someone looks good does not mean that person is marriage material.

The Revelation

THE WOMEN I WAS WITH following the divorce were good, and they taught me a lot about myself. We can often have this impulse to look down on the person we broke up with, place blame on them, or even try to forget about the entire relationship and quickly shift into another. The best thing I did was not to be mad at those women or hold negative thoughts. After the relationships ended, I wished them well and took the time to look at not only what may have gone wrong but also what I did wrong. I needed to be able to look at myself and change not only what I looked for in a relationship but what I provided. The relationships consequently made me a better person and helped me become a better partner.

It does not always seem so clear, but when you step back and look through your past relationships, it can shed some light. I resisted that light for a while but once I opened up to it, I became a new person who changed and adapted. They were not the only people who messed up in the relationship, so did I. I am just happy I could look at them strategically, make changes to myself, and develop the standards that I believed would lead me to find the perfect partner.

AFFIRMATION

Sometimes, put yourself through obstacles to come out on the other side a better person.

PILLAR 9

The refreshing aspect was that I didn't need to get to know her.

Pastor Thorpe

My Story

WHEN I RAN FOR OFFICE for the second time in 2016, one of my advisors thought to put my photograph on the campaign sign. We had great sign locations within Alachua County, and I saw no harm. I was campaigning for maybe six to eight months when I got a friend request on Facebook from a lady I did not know. I knew nothing about her, and I didn't think much of her reaching out. I knew while campaigning that is how people become aware of you, and I had just put up signs with my face attached to them. I felt like this was just someone who saw the sign and wanted to show support. I accepted the friend request and looked through her pictures and life experiences.

One of the main things I noticed was how young and vibrant she was. She was a realtor who graduated from the University of Florida, and she looked to show much promise. I had no romantic interest. I was just accepting a friend request from someone in the community. I was heavily involved in political and community work and thought perhaps this was someone who would be good to work with, but there was no writing to each other or anything. We would react to each other's posts, but I had no idea anything romantic would develop until two years later.

In 2018, she posted some birthday photographs that I felt could be a little compromising for any future endeavors she may have. Part of my drive to get elected to office was to bring other successful young people along and connect them politically, so I sent her a message.

I saw her potential to be a community leader. I wanted to make sure she didn't have any content out there that would hurt her down the road because I thought she was someone who could work on the board for an organization such as United Way, Habitat for Humanity, or the American Cancer Society.

In a rather pointed way, I recommended that she be careful what she posted on social media so that it wouldn't hinder her. She took the photographs down instantly and told me how much she appreciated my interest in her well-being.

After that, we kept in contact. It was nothing serious, we just talked now and again. Some

months into it, we decided to meet to talk about her getting involved in community work, serving on boards, and other organizations she could connect with because my goal was to push her forward. That was the only thing on my mind. I didn't know that she had become interested in me romantically, which I shrugged off instantly once it came to my attention because she was 26 then and I was 44, which in my mind did not compute. It did not enter my mind to date someone that much younger. It was not so much the age difference as it was her age at the time.

I found out later that she had been in relationships with older men, but I felt that was not a bridge I was prepared to cross. I looked to take more of a mentor role in her life, not become a romantic partner, and I told her early on that I was not the man for her. She took it a little rough, but we stayed in touch, and I thought we decided to retain a friendship. We even had special nicknames. She called me "Papa Dearest" and I called her "TT" because she had several nieces and nephews and that's how they referred to her.

We stayed in contact over the years but again, nothing developed beyond our friendship. I didn't know, or at least did not notice, that she still held a romantic interest in me. She did not express it overtly out of respect for me.

We continued to check on each other periodically and then almost constantly during the last four years. At some point, she brought up again her interest in me and her understanding that I had apprehensions about our ages. This was in 2019. She challenged me with the idea that I was missing out on what God had in store for me by worrying about what other people would think.

Still, I made no advances. I just could not wrap my mind around not only being with someone as young as her but also with someone I had developed such a good friendship with by that point. I never saw her as anything more than a good friend. It's hard to shift from sharing funny pictures and stories to flirting and organizing dates.

Despite my repeated rejection of her advancements, we continued to talk about community events, what organizations she could get plugged into, what it cost to serve, and what type of contacts she could make to advance her business. I was just trying to pour into someone with much potential. I thought that with all of my community connections, I could put her in the right position to advance her career.

One day when I had just returned from a trip to Carolina, she wrote to me. It was not uncommon on a Saturday evening for her to send me a message wishing me a great day in church the next day, but this day was different. The conversation lasted into the night, and throughout that conversation, it was like the Lord was speaking to me saying, "Dude, this woman has been here all along. Everything that your heart desires, I have been pouring it into her and revealing it to you. You need to get out of your way and give this a real chance."

I don't make impulsive decisions but that night, I felt overwhelmed by the idea that this person had impressed me with her character and how she carries herself. She was into me. I said, "Lord, if this is the person you are bringing to me, let me broach it with her, and let us take a hard, concrete look at how this can work."

I wrote to her and asked if she would consider getting to know each other differently. I did not see her response until the following day. When she wrote back, she sent a list. She said she would only consider it if, number one, God led me to do so. Number two, I was going to be intentional in how I would pursue the relationship. The third thing was that no one else's opinions would factor into how our relationship developed. I wrote back saying absolutely, and that's where it started.

We started to talk with more intentionality, and I learned the degree to which she had been interested in me throughout the years. I was astonished that there were other people we knew mutually whom she confided in behind the scenes. I had been oblivious to this for all these years. I had no idea that her interest in me was at that level.

We started planning our first date, and I discovered she no longer lived in Gainesville. She instead lived in her hometown of Palatka, which I thought was a good thing. It's good to have some distance when physical attractions are involved, especially when trying to walk upright. So I thought the fact she had moved was healthy and helpful. We planned to meet on a particular Thursday not too long after we decided to take things more seriously in early January. The Tuesday before we were supposed to have our first date, I got COVID-19. That backed up everything, but it was a vital incubation period for us to talk and flesh out more details about each other and our lifelong aspirations.

The refreshing aspect was that I didn't need to get to know her. We had been getting to know each other for years, just not with the anticipation of being in a relationship. I had just been valuing who she was and respecting everything I thought she had to offer. Fast forward and COVID cleared up, so we finally went out. We spent the whole day together on January 20, 2022.

When dating someone for the first time, I'm a question-asking type because I do a lot of counseling and can gauge early on when things are not where they need to be. I asked many questions about thinking, experiences, goals, and desires. I don't believe any question should be off-limits, nor does she. She was very forthright about her desires and anticipation. There were questions I did not need to ask, as she shared automatically.

One of the things we discussed a lot was not only this book project, which I had started years earlier, but the idea of us being able to encourage other couples in the future. We wanted to be the model for other couples to aspire to be. It's funny because this was our first date, but we were already talking about how we wanted to inspire others. That was just how strong our connection was.

From that date on January 20 and throughout the months that followed, we did not miss a single Thursday spending the day together. We planned them out very well. We did horseback riding, ziplining, bowling, hatchet throwing, multiple movies, drive-ins, and eating experiences in Daytona, St. Augustine, Gainesville, and Ocala. It was a whirlwind experience of doing exactly what I prophesied, which I don't say lightly.

I didn't see myself in a dating relationship with someone younger. I said, "Lord, I gave you a whole list of things I want," and the Lord said, "Well, don't get mad at me if I give you everything that you ask for. Just be willing to accept it."

Phoenicha was God's gift to me and from that very first date, I knew this was the woman I would spend the rest of my life with.

The Lesson

LOVE COMES IN MANY FORMS. Often the person you least expect to fall in love with could be the one you end up loving. I was okay at the place I was in life, and this woman was not on my radar.

Over time, she revealed herself to me as the person I had been looking for. I would have never imagined before her that I would be with someone as young as she is. It was impossible in my mind, but she kept up the pressure and clarified that she wanted to be the one for me.

You cannot deny something when it appears obvious. When you see something and get that feeling, you need to look at it. Do not rush into it because that could lead to disaster, but at least explore it more instead of writing it off. I knew she was a good woman when I met her, but I only looked at her as a friend. We would have been together much earlier if I had taken that leap sooner. Always try and give something a chance. You never know what may end up happening.

The Revelation

I TELL DIVORCED PEOPLE to take as much time as possible to heal. I had hardly been by myself as far as having emotional support or companionship since being divorced. I never had an issue with people wanting to get to know me. There was never a shortage of people with whom I felt I could engage in conversation. I just felt the need to be careful and not mislead anyone or make them think we had a romantic relationship when I viewed our connection as a friendship.

I was always careful about how much I allowed people to learn about me based on my life experiences. My pastor would tell me horror stories about ministers who had been either manipulated by people or situations where women may not have been genuine and put pastors in compromising positions. They either threatened pastors with that compromise or it became apparent their interest in that pastor was sort of clout chasing. That meant there would not be a long-term relationship based on genuine intentions. I brought all of those cautions with me to my married life and certainly brought them to single life after divorce.

For me, the ability to let my guard down with her made her feel different from any of the other girls. I do not think

I noticed this at the beginning, but a looseness came about once she came into my life. I did not feel like I had to worry about her deceiving me, playing me, or doing anything of that nonsense. Ultimately that helped us excel in something serious because, for the first time since getting into the dating world, I felt I had met someone who made me feel comfortable. I do not think I was cognizant of this initially, but I am indeed glad I came to the realization.

AFFIRMATION

When you sit back and wait, God reveals to you exactly what you were looking for.

PILLAR 10

My church resonates with my happiness,
so they welcomed her with open arms
once they saw the joy she brought me.

Pastor Thorpe

My Story

THINGS MOVED VERY QUICKLY from a historical perspective after that first date. Our first date was January 20, and I bought Phoenicha a ring–her dream ring–the very next day. She had taken a picture of the ring set years prior but didn't know how to find it. That was alright though. I found it for her.

It was like a rocket ship after that. My family was proud that I was able to find someone. They had seen the years of trauma I had been through and the pain it had caused me. They also saw the renewed smile on my face that was the direct result of my romantic relationship. I am sure it made them aware of how special this woman was to me.

Family members were not the only people who saw a change in me. Members of my congregation did as well. I am going into my 27th year of serving my church. Members have seen me go through many huge events over the years. From the separation and divorce from my ex-wife to running for office, dating my current wife, and the passing of my father in 2019, they have seen me at the bottom more than once. It was never like I was an angry or stiff person, but I think it was obvious my focus was sometimes somewhere else.

But from the moment Phoenicha came into my life and I introduced her to the church, I think they saw a huge transition in me. With her, I let my guard down and relaxed in a way I had not been able to do in a long time. The church saw that shift, and many pointed that out to both me and Phoenicha, which I think helped her transition into the church.

My church resonates with my happiness, so they welcomed her with open arms once they saw the joy she brought me. Case in point, congregation members threw her a first-class bridal shower, hiring a private caterer and decorating the church's fellowship hall space. It was just a full afternoon of excitement for her. Then, the male leaders of the church had a bachelor's gathering for me. It was going on at the same time as her bridal shower. About two hours after the women's party started, they finished at the church and came to the house where the guys entertained me. The women transformed my celebration, and we spent the next two hours there. It was our families, the church families, men and women, just celebrating us as a couple. It was one of the most memorable events of our lives.

They have always been there and for that, I am very thankful. I have invested so much of who I am into helping singles prepare for marriage and helping married couples be as attentive to each other as they should be. To see it come full circle for me was like new air for me and them. They celebrated with me as I embarked on a new journey with Phoenicha.

The Lesson

THE BIGGEST THING I have learned since falling in love again is that God can catch you by surprise. When I look back, I realize that I am normally a very calculated person. If I am planning an event and I know the event is 12 months away, I will start making plans 12 months in advance. I will anticipate where the hiccups will be, looking through step by step for potential problems. With this relationship and engagement, I took myself out of every comfort zone. I became more vulnerable and open to doing things I never envisioned.

Phoenicha has been so attentive to my desires and interests that she has allowed me to be open and vulnerable. My heart has felt safe knowing that I am connected to a person who cannot only handle who I am but can handle whomever God will transform me into over time. Having the congregation see and acknowledge the changes in me has also been astounding.

To the person holding out hope, I say to keep the faith. Wait until you find that person who transforms you, who complements you in every possible way, the person who when people see you with them says, "Wow, you are a different person." I just needed to be patient, and you do as well. That person is out there waiting for you, and God is preparing them to come into your life.

The Revelation

I AM ALWAYS extremely careful about who I introduce to my congregation and my family. These are two critical groups in my life and if you are going to be a part of my life, it is helpful that they get to know and engage with you. I never got the impression from any church members that they were worried about our relationship from a longevity standpoint. They were supportive from the very beginning, which reaffirmed the trust I needed to place in them.

They trust that I know what I am doing, and they know I would never bring someone around if I was not serious about that person. It is a true family I have been able to cultivate at my church, and I have to be one of the most fortunate pastors out there. I always knew that, but seeing their reaction when I told them about Phoenicha and our engagement only provided further reassurance.

AFFIRMATION

Keep your circle filled with loving friends and family.

PILLAR 11

The whole experience was priceless.

Pastor Thorpe

My Story

WE BEGAN PLANNING the wedding for July 16, 2022.

The venue was the biggest decision that consumed our time at the beginning. Phoenicha had always wanted to get married at the Baughman Center at the University of Florida, but the campus was completing a project to replace the siding on the building. They could not guarantee when it would be available because we were initially looking at the end of the year between September and December. So we looked at dates before the construction project began. In addition, Pho, my wife's nickname, mentioned how she believed she heard from God that we were to be "one at one o'clock." That made it imperative that whatever we did, the ceremony was to start at one. This created a little issue regarding finding a date with a time slot to accommodate the wedding.

Once the Baughman Center was reserved for July 16, we began to search for the reception venue.

We wanted it near the Baughman Center as well but learned that was not feasible. We considered having the event at the church where I pastor and also considered the Cade Museum, which is where I proposed. I previously served on the museum's board of directors. We settled on the Best Western Gateway Grand.

We did several tastings and locked in the food and beverage before focusing on the decorations. When we realized a local decorator wanted a nonrefundable $500 to simply discuss a plan, we took a step back to determine what exactly we wanted. We used the wedding ceremony of Pastor Marvin Winans, who we both looked up to and who had recently married, as a basis for what decorations we wanted.

Things turned out slightly more pricey than I originally intended, but that was fine. I was more interested in finding someone to bring what Pho and I envisioned to life. The woman we chose to take charge of the decorations provided a list of preferred vendors, including a florist who I called directly. She partnered with an event decorator who laid out table covers and the chargers that went under the settings.

We had a photographer booked and in place. We also hired a separate videographer for the ceremony and reception, one who had an interesting backstory. All the companies I contacted just wanted to produce highlight videos that would be 60 seconds to two-and-a-half minutes long. I wanted the entire wedding and reception recorded, so I contacted a friend who used to be a production manager at Cox Cable. He said he didn't usually do weddings, but we met and he said it would be an honor for him to record our wedding. He would use five or six cameras and said I could not pay him to do it. He said while he was going through his divorce, he would watch me preach on Facebook, and he started quoting my sermons back to me. That just really touched my heart.

We hired a "day of" event planner who Pho reached out to and who became more engaged 30 days before the wedding. We had an elaborate meeting and walked through all the details. We did two walk-throughs of the wedding and reception venues. Her services included reviewing all contracts, so she had a copy of every contract we signed. She was to communicate directly with all the vendors for the wedding or reception.

One of the details she caught very early was that the Best Western had booked us in the wrong time slot for the reception, which was a blow for us. It would have been virtually impossible for us to have the reception given everything had to be over by 3 p.m. and the wedding was at 1 p.m.

I have worked with the Best Western chain before on several things. My 20th pastoral anniversary celebration was held there. I was taken aback by the error and had to take responsibility for it. I signed the contract with the times on it without actually looking at it carefully. We learned they were trying to do two events on the same day, and someone decided that the second event would take priority over our reception.

I called management to try and remedy the situation, but that did not help because the manager was a pain to work with. Staff apologized and worked hard to find us a solution, but this was maybe five weeks before the wedding, so time was of the essence. They had a second venue on site available, so we planned to eat and have the preliminary pieces of the reception in their large ballroom, then transition everyone to the pre-reception room for the toastings, the bouquet and garter toss, and cake cutting. Arranging the second place was challenging because it all happened at the last minute.

The florist and the decorator had to go above and beyond the call of duty the night before the wedding. I was caught off guard when I visited the venue for the reception because nothing looked like we had planned. The tablecloths did not go to the floor. You could see the framing of the tables. I was not at the point of having a meltdown when I saw this, but I was not pleased. I told the decorators I didn't care how much money it would cost, we needed to get the venue looking right.

From there, they went into overdrive mode. Their finished product, from a visual perspective, was three to four times greater than what we had contracted for, so I was pleased with the decorator. She did a beautiful job. Several times throughout that Friday night and a couple of times on Saturday morning, they brought in additional staffing and made multiple trips to bring in different things. They made it work in both spaces.

We had to pay the florist a little more because they had to order additional plants, which they could not get at regular prices. That hurt the pocketbook a little, but I would have been so embarrassed by what they were doing beforehand that I did not care what the price was. It needed to be done correctly.

Another issue we had was with the vehicle we rented for the ceremony. Pho wanted to use a white Phantom Rolls Royce to bring her to the ceremony. I found a dealership that had the Cullinan, an oversized Rolls Royce SUV. I secured it in February and paid in full. Everything was set for it to be delivered to the hotel. I had someone from the church who would chauffeur us around, so everything looked set and ready to go.

The "day of" planner in charge of contacting our vendors did not speak to the car people. I was communicating with them and we spoke two weeks prior to the wedding, as well as a day or so before the ceremony. While visiting the reception venue, I got an email at 5:52 p.m. THE DAY

BEFORE the wedding saying the car reservation could not be fulfilled. I was devastated. That was less than 24 hours before the wedding. What was I to do? I started brainstorming some options, and it came to me.

I had done a lot of business with a Mercedes dealership, so I called the salesperson, left him a voicemail, and told him I was in a bind. I did not hear from him because he had already left for the day, so I decided to drive to the dealership. I was standing in the lobby where cars were on display. I saw a white G Wagon with a red interior. It was not the car Pho originally wanted, but I thought it was as close as I could get under the circumstances. I got inside the building and told them, "I could not get your sales guy on the phone. Could you get him on the phone?" This was urgent, and I knew at least he would attempt to help me.

They tried a few times, but we couldn't get him. His sister also worked at the dealership but had been off for several days because she was not feeling well. I found out a couple of days later that she had been diagnosed with COVID-19. I called her, and you could hear in her voice that she was not feeling well. I told her what we were up against, and she promised to do all she could to reach her brother and make it work.

I waited in the lobby of the dealership, which I didn't know had closed for the day, hoping for the sister to pull a miracle. Finally, they reached the salesman. He spoke with the general manager, who said he couldn't rent me a car. He then said that if one of their employees was willing to chauffeur us, they could make it work.

We couldn't do the white G Wagon because he had sold it two hours earlier and couldn't put any additional miles on it, but they had a black one. So we had paid $2,400 for a one-day rental of the Rolls Royce, but we got the G Wagon instead. The rental fee was promptly refunded.

The sales guy who helped me with the general manager offered to chauffeur us on the wedding day, even though he had people scheduled to come in and buy cars that Saturday morning. He brought the car, picked Pho up from the Hilton Hotel, took her to the ceremony, waited until the ceremony was over, and took us to the Best Western.

Pho did not have many outlandish requests for the wedding, but she really wanted the Rolls Royce to drive her up for the wedding. I worked to make all her requests come true, but when I had to switch cars, I thought it appropriate to present this news with something special. Her absolute favorite meal on the planet is called Asun. It is an African dish that means spicy goat meat. She likes to buy it from this restaurant around Atlanta. A couple of days before the wedding I contacted my nephew, who was coming in for the wedding from Atlanta, and learned he lived about 40 minutes from the restaurant. He graciously arranged his trip to include stopping by the restaurant to pick up her favorite dish and bought multiple servings for her.

I thought having the food in hand would soften the blow, and that was what happened. Still, she was taken aback that the car was not available because we booked it so far in advance and had already paid for it.

By Friday night, Pho was at the hotel where she would stay. We were just waiting for the ceremony the next day. Everything and everyone appeared ready to go for the ceremony. We left all of the details for the day in the hands of our planner.

As the ceremony began, Pho finally entered the building. She looked stunning. The dress was phenomenal and she wore it with a matching cape. I was totally blown away. And there we were, bound in Holy Matrimony and "one at one," just as we had planned.

Pho often says, "The juice must be worth the squeeze." I believe, all in all, the juice was worth the squeeze even though a lot was going on behind the scenes that folks did not know about. The whole experience was priceless and created the union I had been seeking with my soulmate.

All of the challenges I faced before meeting Pho were how God cultivated me and prepared me for my marriage. He put me through a tough first marriage and three separate relationships to help me develop the knowledge to handle my subsequent marriage. I had the knowledge and skills needed to have a successful relationship and happy life with my wife.

The Lesson

I HAVE WITNESSED many marriages, both as a pastor and as a bystander, and it is a different feeling when you are the one getting married. You have to make sure every little detail is taken care of when it's your wedding. The lesson I learned from this experience is to ensure everyone involved in the ceremony is on the same page. Ensure the people you hire are fully competent in what they are doing. They must have the right experience and mindset to ensure everything goes smoothly.

Even when you think you have hired the right people, triple- and quadruple-check everything and everyone because anything can and may go wrong.

I also have to say that through this experience, God had to look down on my wife and me. So many things were coming up and at the most inconvenient moment. We went in thinking everything was set and ready to go, but something kept disrupting the plan. He had to look down on us that day. It just shows that when He wants something to happen, He will make sure it occurs.

The Revelation

YOU DON'T NEED to be a pastor or a bystander to know that weddings are a beautiful moment as two people unite their lives, but there is a different feeling when it is your wedding. I have never felt the joy I felt once I married my wife Pho. This feeling is hard to explain and I think hard to replicate. Do not get me wrong, it was stressful. But the moment we said, "I do," this tremendous weight lifted off my shoulders. I could look at her as my wife and know we will spend the rest of our lives together. Our love is this unbreakable bond that remains so pure today.

Love is one of the purest things we humans can experience in a lifetime. I may have given up on love at one point in my life, but it was never because of my hatred of the idea of love or marriage. I have always been a proponent of love in my personal and professional life. My second marriage reaffirmed why love, relationships, and marriage mean so much to me and why I want people worldwide to experience what I have experienced.

I had several moments when I wanted to pull my hair out, but I never had a second from the day of our first date when I doubted I wanted to spend the rest of my life with her. Seeing her walk down that aisle confirmed that I was making the right decision.

AFFIRMATION

When love is a priority in your life, it will lead to some of the most wonderful experiences.

PILLAR 12

To find a lifelong partner, you must be strategic.

Pastor Thorpe

My Story

TO THIS DAY, I love the institution of marriage and am living proof that happiness can be found with the right person. I do not want what I went through in my first marriage to be an example of why marriage is not a viable option for people. I found someone I love dearly and who loves me back, and we cemented that love through marriage. But it does take effort and dedication to find someone you want to spend the rest of your life with.

I believe three absolute factors must be present if a marriage is to be successful. I try to counsel people to keep this in mind when they are thinking of getting married or looking for someone to marry. I view it as a stool that needs three legs. One of the three may get a little shaky, but if that happens, you can pivot to the other two until the third leg gets better. If two are shaky, you only have one leg to stand on, which will be difficult.

The first characteristic is maturity. In a relationship, maturity is having the ability to say I am committed to meeting my partner's needs. If you have an internal problem doing so, you must address those struggles instead of saying, "If you do better, then I will do better." That is immature.

If maturity means I am committed to meeting your needs, then I oppose selfishness. If a person getting married is selfish and unwilling to meet the legitimate needs of their spouse, then that person is not fit for marriage. They will put the needs of their spouse to the side at any given moment based on their desires or frustrations. They are going to settle into their selfishness and simply refuse to change. So maturity is the first part.

The second leg is compatibility. I believe spouses need to share. They do not have to agree on everything, but their thinking should move in the same direction. When I counsel couples, I ask a whole lot of questions. What are their philosophies on children? How many children? What career sacrifices are they willing to make to raise their children? How will they discipline the children? Will they allow their children to date at a certain age?

I get couples to flesh out as much as possible. We talk about debt, finances, in-laws, and communication. Then I do an important exercise with every couple to help them determine their capabilities. I believe all people fall into three different categories regarding their thinking: Job people, Career people, or Dreamers. There is nothing wrong with any of the three. They are all important, but understanding where you lie will help you find a compatible partner.

When you ask what a job person does for a living they will say, for example, "I work at Amazon." They're expressing that their connection with their job ends at 5:30 p.m. when they get off. At that point, they don't want to hear anything about Amazon or look at the uniform.

Career people have whatever they do for a living as part of their DNA, and they may do it at 11 p.m. It's not that it takes away from home life, it's just a part of them. I don't think there is anything wrong with the two. The danger comes when you start mixing them and one spouse is a job person while the other is a career person.

Unless the job person is mature, they will grow a sense of envy or animosity toward the other person's career. They will say, "Well, I get off at 5:30, and I don't think about my job. You got off at 5:30, and here it is 11 p.m. and you are still looking up things connected to what you do." Or the job person will tell the career person, "You spend too much time on your work." Anybody who marries an attorney, for example, cannot assume their spouse's brain turns off at 5 p.m. I consequently recommend getting two job people together so you're both off at 5 or two career people who can identify with the fact that they will both be working on something.

Then there are the dreamers. These are creative people in art, sports, and entertainment. Lord knows we need these people. What I have found with dreamers is that they can make it on very little financially. They are the kind of people who rent a room in a friend's house and are willing to invest all their resources into their dreams. Life would be boring if we didn't have these people, but the problem comes when you get a job person and a dreamer together. That job person will support the dreamer in those first six to 12 months. But when you spend all your money on your dreams and not the bills, that job person will say, "You need a 9-5 job." The dreamer will say, "You knew I was this way when we got together. Why are you trying to kill my dream?"

At some point, the career person will say, "I know this is your dream, but what about taking some courses at night to have something to fall back on?" The dreamer will say, "Here you are, trying to change me." The same tension arises when you mix a job person with a career person.

The third leg is chemistry, and that's the physical aspect. It is my firm belief that people should not get married to folks they're not attracted to and do not want to be with physically. Both are essential not only from a biblical point of view but also based on the mistakes people make, especially church folks. Many Christian folks say the next relationship they get into won't be about looks. I don't think that's a good idea. You should not overlook the physical aspects because even the most spiritual person will not always behave super spiritual. If you're going through a rough patch, at a minimum, you need to like looking at and touching each other.

So maturity, chemistry, and compatibility are all three essential.

I am convinced that younger people can find a lifelong soulmate or maintain a relationship if they hold on to these three principles. If they can mature into the relationship and understand what they're looking for from a compatibility standpoint, they are positioned well to have a long, healthy relationship.

For some people, these rules may seem a little too rigid. Many people want to feel free and believe they can be with whomever they want and that as long as there's love, it will all work out. Love is a component of any relationship, but it will not save a failing relationship.

To find a lifelong partner, you must be strategic. You must ask questions to understand the person you are contemplating spending the rest of your life with. You do not want to walk down the aisle and then get to know your spouse.

Marriage is nothing to play with. I was young and in love, but I did not put in the work to see that my first wife was not the person I should be with. That is why we divorced. I did it the right way before my second marriage. I took the time, built rigid standards, and sought the three things that are required to have a successful marriage. God brought to me the woman of my dreams and will empower you to find your soulmate as well.

The Lesson

MARRIAGE IS BEAUTIFUL and could be the best experience in your life, but some things must be in place to make a marriage work. Many couples look at each other and conclude that they are good-looking and that is all they need to make their relationship last. That is not what makes a marriage work. Love, chemistry, and compatibility are vital. While not all three need to be displayed in the most robust form, at least some aspect of each must be present in the relationship for it to be healthy. If you have been divorced or had a recent breakup, I also think it is necessary to understand which of the three was not in place. The fact one was missing may have been the reason your relationship ended.

It's never fun to put a lot of thinking into a relationship when you are just getting to know another person, but you have to if you want something that will last a long time. We all like to think we know what we are doing but truthfully, we don't. That's because we do not ask the right questions and approach dating the right way. If you want something wholesome that will last, then you must ask difficult questions and at least be attracted to the person. It's not easy, but it is necessary. There is no magic bullet to make a relationship last the rest of your life, but you can do a few things to put the odds in your favor and have a marriage with a happy outcome.

The Revelation

THE WAY I CAME to these conclusions about marriage and divorce was not just because I read the Bible a few more times but because I noticed what was lacking in my relationships. When you are in a relationship, at least initially, you begin to think it is the best and this is the person for you. It is only when the relationship ends that you realize what is missing.

That is how I came to these conclusions. I saw the voids in my life and discovered that if I had done the necessary work to weed out those things in the early stages of my relationships, I might have never married my first wife. But I didn't have the knowledge yet.

I acquired it through the relationships I had before marrying Pho. I didn't think I was learning anything at the moment, but when I took my emotions out of it and really thought about it, I understood what was missing. By the time I met my Pho, I had the standard and discipline to know what I wanted, what questions to ask, what I was not going to put up with, and the ability to understand if she was right for me.

During breakups, you need to look at what worked and what did not. In the beginning, there will be a level of anger and sadness, but look past that. I found my wife today because I put in the extra work to see my flaws and set my priorities. That is how I found the most special woman in the world.

AFFIRMATION

Love is waiting for all of us.

Conclusion

> Marriage is an institution that has
> endured the test of time.
>
> Pastor Thorpe

WHEN YOU LISTEN TO or read my sermon about Christ turning water into wine, I want you to understand the meaning of love. I want you to learn how to find love and when you find it, how to maintain it. It's easy to get into a relationship but it is harder to keep that relationship going for the rest of your life.

It's also easy to leave a relationship and fall into a dark place. Love is sticky, and it can hurt. It can also be one of the most beautiful things you have ever experienced. When you are going through bad times or have the displeasure of going through a divorce, do not get discouraged by love. Doing so will lead to a painful life. Love is the thing that brings us out of a dark place. Marriage is an institution that has endured the test of time. It makes us smile or keeps us young. You need to believe in love because sometimes, in this crazy world, love is all we have.

Focus on redemption. Even with my current marital status, I am still a pastor who divorced. Going through that, I could have wrapped up my career and accepted that I no longer had the right to preach the word. There were probably some people who thought that was exactly what I should do.

Not only did I not give up on love, I did not give up on myself. I came out of that dark place I was in for so many years better than ever, and now I am happier than ever. Even when you are going through a dark time, redemption and second chances are still possible. God's mission for you has not ended, it is still progressing. You just have to stay true and open to what He offers you.

Afterword:
A Recipe for Marriage

> A recipe for marriage is as sweet
> or as bitter as the chefs.
>
> Pastor Thorpe

PRIOR TO WRITING THIS BOOK, I had not rediscovered love. Now that the book has been completed, God has made me whole by blessing me with an amazing wife and adorable son. It is of utmost importance to me to demonstrate how we approach our relationship and honor God. We make sure He has a seat at the table. We showcase how He allowed us to cultivate our relationship, and we demonstrate how our marriage has flourished because we keep God first. We sat down for a candid interview prior to the completion of this book. I thought it befitting to share our answers with you. May they bless your spirit.

How do you prioritize spiritual growth individually and as a couple to strengthen your connection to God?

FIRST LADY THORPE

I make sure that I prioritize my daily devotional, Bible reading, and my prayer. Typically, when I go on my walks, I make sure that I don't talk to anyone on the phone. I will have my baby with me but that is it. It is my quiet time for this reflection to see where I'm at, or if I'm feeling like, "Hey, I'm lacking in an area" and it's something that can initially be resolved between God and myself. So I'm very big on it. Can I work this out between God and myself before I talk to my husband? That way, it's less likely that I will need to discuss things with him. Not that I can't, but the fact that it's just one less thing that I'm bringing him to discuss considering he's my husband and my pastor. So I make sure I prioritize my daily devotional, prayer, and Bible reading. When I go on my walks, I hone in and talk to God by myself.

PASTOR THORPE

It's virtually automatic. I mean, because so much of what I must do vocationally focuses on being spiritually centered, it's a constant for me. I believe in practicing what I preach in that sense. The new Bible study series I'm starting deals with being centered and focused, so it's not a struggle for us to stay focused spiritually. It's just such a constant.

What specific practices do you incorporate in your daily lives to keep God at the center of your marriage?

FIRST LADY THORPE

As a collective, I would say prayer together and individually.

PASTOR THORPE

We pray together, and we talk a lot around the clock.

How do you rely on your faith in God's guidance to navigate difficulties within your relationships?

FIRST LADY THORPE

I would say what I initially did was pause and immediately talk to God myself. One of the things God laid on my heart, and I didn't know if I could be this type of person, is being mindful of premeditated things. It's clear as day. What that means is usually you're already planning your response when someone says something to you and you're immediately going to respond in a way that is bad to move forward or it's going to cause additional conflict.

So I always pause and ask, "Is this response right? How can I self-reflect?" That's allowing God to convict me or highlight things.

I just lean to God and say "Hey, is this me?" I self-reflect, meditate on it, and then I'm quiet because I want to be strategic about speaking slowly. Then basically, I see what I have grabbed in my Easter egg basket from all of the teachings that I have learned or nuggets I got from sermons along the way. I take what I already have and see how to apply it to make sure I don't make the situation worse.

And then at some point, he's very good because he'll initiate most of the time. He will say, "Can we discuss this," or "When is a good time for us?" Yesterday, we weren't our best selves or slightly different. What a good time to have a conversation, honestly. Every time he initiates that, I'm thankful because I'll just see what he says. I've made it a point to be open whenever he opens the door to communicate about the situation. Sometimes It's just a misunderstanding. I thought he meant this and he thought I meant that. So I rely on my faith to say I don't have to make this as difficult, but I always try to do self-reflection.

PASTOR THORPE

Looking at life through a biblical lens, I believe in considering the warnings in the word, such as the promises, the principles, and the examples. Based on all of those, I try to filter everything that we say.

How do you ensure that your communication reflects the values and teachings that you hold dear to your faith?

FIRST LADY THORPE

Like the Golden Rule, you treat others how you want to be treated. I pause. Hey, it's communication. I have to watch my tone to know I have the right attitude. When you have a person who has time for you and communicates very well with you, it makes you want to reciprocate that. If you truly love a person, it's like, "Hey, I need to be mindful of how I present things to you." With my communication. I'm slow to make sure I first think about what he said and ask clarifying questions. I do so in a good manner because I am simply looking for clarity. I also remember being mindful of a premeditated attitude. Growing up, I was always quick at the mouth, getting in trouble in school and with my mom because my comeback was quick. So now I ensure my communication is the opposite of that as I first pause to understand and ask clarifying questions and know I need to reciprocate how he treats me. He always talks to me very gently, so I talk to him gently.

PASTOR THORPE

Maintaining mutual respect means that there are no big "I's" or little "you's". She is just as much a child of God as I am, and I never take that for granted.

Have you established shared goals and dreams that align with your spiritual beliefs? How do these goals contribute to the strength of your marriage?

FIRST LADY THORPE

Yes, but not fully in-depth. It's funny because we were just saying, "Hey, we need to sit down and dive into that." What we've agreed on is that we're in such a good flow, and this is why I brought it to him. You have to show intentionality. So, it goes preliminarily based on wherever we are. Dating, of course, but as far as that next level of life and a definitive timeline, not so much.

PASTOR THORPE

We both have several goals and with our new baby, we're implementing them and discovering more. It's a healthy, challenging time for us as we raise our child and everything that encompasses.

Regarding the second part, I think the more we focus on cultivating a new life, the more thankful I am. We had about a year of it just being the two of us in married life, and now the baby is here. When two spiritually mature people have to pull together to decide how to raise another person effectively, it creates a path to stay focused spiritually.

How do you support each other's spiritual journeys and encourage growth in your shared faith?

FIRST LADY THORPE

We're always human, holding each other accountable even in the smallest things. So if it's something where he gets upset, I remind him to catch himself or just to be more grounded. After his sermons on Wednesdays and Sundays, I tell him what I learned, that I'm so proud of him, or note how he connected thoughts. I let him know I see the effort that he puts in with his preparation.

PASTOR THORPE

I think one of the other unique things about us is we work together in the ministry, just not so much on the preaching side. She works on the media side by making things look good and sound good. I have a lot of spiritual planning for what God has given me to pour into the church on any given Wednesday or Sunday. She's a part of that on the front end as well as on the back end. I think it builds a strength that is sustained in itself.

How do you handle conflicts or disagreements in a way that honors your commitment to a God-centered marriage?

PASTOR THORPE

I think that for us, it's based on never forgetting that more than the fact that she's my spouse, she's also God's child. I would never do anything to disrespect or harm God's child. That's why I hold myself to that same standard. I don't take her for granted. I am careful about what I do in or outside of her presence because I genuinely fear God. So, whatever that disagreement is, it's just more of collectively working through it.

How do you both actively integrate God into your daily lives to ensure your marriage remains centered on Him?

FIRST LADY THORPE

He prepares messages and I work on the media side. He forwards everything to me in advance, so I get to be somewhat of a first-take. While he is preparing, I can review it. On the front end, I take care of it on the media side but also on the back end. I'm able to review what it is that he's going to be preaching about, and then go back to see how the media looks at the production stage and the live stream. So I'm listening to it again. Also, I sit quietly beside him on the couch whenever he is studying and preparing. I'm kind of watching over and seeing what it is that he's preparing, but also just staying in my alone time with God. During my walks, I don't like to talk to anyone. My Bible reading, my prayer, and my daily devotional keep me going spiritually from an individual level.

PASTOR THORPE

One of the fun things about our life and our church is that there are three messages that I have to prepare for every week. I am a life skills kind of preacher. I believe in dealing with things that people face every day, and I am constantly in the mode of building other people. First I am a partaker of what I'm trying to use to impact other people. For example, the last two sermons on Sunday morning have dealt specifically with dating, marriage, and family. So yeah, we're constantly surrounded by spiritual focus, but it's a cultivated focus. We're not trying to teach others to do something we are not exposed to, so it helps keep things focused and centered.

Can you share specific examples of how you prioritize prayer and worship together as a couple?

PASTOR THORPE

We genuinely worship together every Sunday and are unique in this sense. We both have to be at church very early. We are prepared essentially with the sermon before we ever get there because we worked on it together, one on the media side and the other on the preparation and delivery side. So, we are immersed in prayer and worship all the time.

How do you navigate the challenges of busy schedules and external pressures to ensure your commitment to God remains unwavering in your relationship?

PASTOR THORPE

It's not that our schedules are very busy, but they are very demanding. From Sunday afternoon until Wednesday afternoon of each week, I'm in Jacksonville as a caregiver for my 96-year-old mom. The other times, of course, I'm in Gainesville. One of the things that we practice wholeheartedly is 99% of the time that I'm in Gainesville, we are together. I don't take that for granted. I work as hard as I can to make certain that when I'm in, I'm in.

We share our meals, so I take that part very seriously. Then we talk around the clock. We're constantly communicating, either on the phone or via text or through sharing things back and forth on social media. We talk about every little thing, from picking out shoes to what new thing we want to buy for the baby. I think that is key. Sometimes one spouse may consider something more important than the other, and they kind of leave everything else to the other person. We don't do that. Our habit and practice has been to work through everything together, even the most minute details so that everybody stays on the same page. We are constantly sharing opinions and valuing each other's okayness.

I think our commitment to each other, in a way, reflects our commitment to God just because He ordained marriage and how He outlined it in us. We keep those principles in mind and prioritize the love and respect that we have for each other continuously. We make sure we're staying connected through constant communication. If you prioritize your relationship with God, you're constantly communicating with Him. Your respect for Him dictates how you live your life and honor Him. We try to mirror that in our relationship.

But in what ways do you intentionally incorporate spiritual practices such as reading scriptures or attending religious services to strengthen your bond with God and each other?

PASTOR THORPE

I think it's a gift for us. As we're sharing this, I'm reflecting on the fact that, unfortunately, there are a lot of pastors who don't feel comfortable sharing things like their sermons with anybody, let alone their spouse. That's a tall wall to climb. The healthy vulnerability that it creates allows me to know that my wife not only respects the calling on my life, she respects my dedication to empowering and impacting people. She doesn't give me any grief about expressing that level of love and concern for the people I've been called to serve.

How do you approach decision-making as a couple seeking God's guidance and wisdom in the choices you make for your marriage and family?

FIRST LADY THORPE

We think about things individually, but as he said, we discuss even the smallest details. God is always in our decision-making because we're keeping each other in the loop, even with the smallest details. Whenever I bring something to him or he's thinking about something, he's brought it to me. He'll always say if we can't decide at the moment, I'll give it some prayerful consideration. If it's something vice versa, I'll say the same just because that's his wording. We bring each other everything, big and little, and then also just have a moment to pray about it and see what is best for us.

PASTOR THORPE

I agree, and I am so indebted. I'm telling you, I appreciate it so much that things do not blindside me. I think a lot of it involves mutual respect and a mutual submission that says number one, we are doing life together. Whatever the decision is, there's no value in it if it offends the other person. The fact that we do get to talk about things like Christmas ornaments and she sends me pictures of them before she buys them. I love that I eat that up because the flip side would be that these are our Christmas ornaments, and you just need to deal with them instead of what works for us. And I think this is a good point for couples in general. When you don't have that—when one person says I'm not running anything by you or when the other person says that when you run things by me I'm going to be dismissive as if the question was pointless—you should have never brought it to me in the first place. I think that creates a dilemma for both sides when things are brought up. They aren't received in the right way. I'm very thankful for the level of communication that we have. And I think it's a level of playing it safe, which is a good thing. You have to take the risk, but I think we play it safe. There is nothing too small of a detail that we feel we shouldn't run by the other person.

Have you established boundaries to protect the sacredness of your relationship with God among the demands of everyday life?

PASTOR THORPE

Certainly. This is true for anybody who deals with others. You must have several boundaries. One of the things that may help someone like me after having gone through an unsuccessful marriage is that you learn a lot along the way. You learn how not to make some of the same mistakes you may have made or how to avoid red flags better than in the past. I think a lot of it is kind of experience-based.

And again, thankfully, we're around each other so much. We just don't tolerate foolishness. People face many issues when allowing others into their personal space or business. I think we're both very private people individually. We were that way before we got together, and we just enjoy the fact that we get to share everything.

How do you share your faith with each other, fostering an environment where spiritual growth is not only individual but also a shared journey in your faith?

PASTOR THORPE

I think a part of it is discussing strengths and weaknesses or struggles. Transparency creates an environment where you have to trust someone. They have to handle your transparency. One of the things, specifically in the years of friendship we had before we ever decided to date and marry, was that she just handled our friendship so well and never crossed any boundaries. We did not make each other feel uncomfortable in any way, so I knew a whole lot on the front end about her love and respect for me. I certainly would never do anything to disrespect or harm her, even when we would just be friends.

FIRST LADY THORPE

I would just say we treat each other well and Biblically do our best. We treat each other with mutual love and respect. For each of us, the priority is to build up our relationship as a whole.

About the Author

KEVIN THORPE has devoted much of his adult life to strengthening marriages and families. He has hosted numerous marriage retreats with titles such as "How To Get On The Love Boat and Stay Off The Titanic," "God's Promise of Miracle Marriages," and "'Meet' Me In The Bedroom." He holds an associate's degree, bachelor's degree, and master's degree in pastoral ministries. He has served as the senior pastor of Faith Church in Gainesville, Florida, since April 1998. His community and civic involvement have been extensive, serving dozens of local and statewide organizations. Kevin owns and operates The Captain's Closet, a custom clothing company that provides premium suits for a broad range of clients across the nation.

He also knows first-hand what it is like to be a loving Christian and still find himself divorced after more than two decades of marriage to his high school sweetheart. His passion is to remove the stigma of divorce from Christians who have unsuccessfully fought in silence through a difficult and failing marriage. He is proudly married to Phoenicha J. Hires and welcomed the arrival of their first baby, Kevin W. Thorpe II, in April 2024.

www.ingramcontent.com/pod-product-compliance
Lightning Source LLC
Chambersburg PA
CBHW042030050526
44107CB00128B/1489/J